ROYAL HORTICULTURAL SOCIETY

PRACTICAL
CACTUS
& SUCCULENT
BOOK

ROYAL HORTICULTURAL SOCIETY

PRACTICAL
CACTUS
& SUCCULENT
BOOK

FRAN BAILEY
ZIA ALLAWAY

CONTENTS

INTRODUCTION

Cacti and succulents are iconic. Symbols of 21st-century living, they populate the windowsills of urban flats and family homes alike, decorate shop displays and office desks, and have quite simply taken over social media. Almost every variety has some unique characteristic that grabs your attention, be it colourful, fleshy leaves, odd shapes, spiny armour, or dazzling flowers.

As their name suggests, succulents store moisture in their thick, fleshy stems, leaves, or roots. While often grouped separately, cacti are also a type of succulent, and are equally adapted to survive the most inhospitable conditions on Earth.

Thanks to this reputation for being hard to kill, these resilient, low-maintenance plants are the ideal choice for first-time indoor gardeners of all ages. Those who have kept cacti and succulents for years, meanwhile, know that it is almost

impossible to limit yourself to just one or two plants: with so many varieties to choose from, and with it being so easy to propagate new plants from existing specimens, your collection can soon grow and grow in more ways than one.

But, once you've amassed an huge assortment of weird and wonderful cacti and succulents, how do you make the most of them? What's the most effective way to display them and show them off at their best? What eye-catching projects can you create with them? How do you encourage them to flower, or coax them back to health if they start to look unwell?

This book has everything you need to nurture your plants and keep them looking their best. Let it be your inspiration and your guide as you care for your collection, and before too long you'll understand just what makes cacti and succulents so uniquely iconic.

DESIGNING
WITH PLANTS

DESIGNING WITH
CHARACTER

Whether compact or towering, spiky or smooth, striped or speckled, every cactus and succulent has some curious yet appealing quality that gives it character. Before you design your display, think about your plants' characteristics. This will help when you curate your arrangements later on.

Sansevieria cylindrica: tall, spiky, smooth

Opuntia microdasys: furry, irregular, yellow-toned

Euphorbia ingens: tall and branching

Euphorbia tirucalli: smooth and branching

Opuntia vestita: small, furry, branching

Echeveria: rosette-shaped, blue-green, flowering

Pilocereus pachycladus: spiny, columnar, blue-green

Curio rowleyanus: trailing, bead-like leaves

Sansevieria trifasciata: tall, glossy, patterned

Rhipsalis baccifera: wild and trailing

Epiphyllum anguliger: wavy, trailing, bright green leaves

Lepismium monacanthum: smooth, trailing stems

Haworthia 'Big Band': small, spiky, striped

Rebutia: round, neat, compact

Cotyledon tomentosa: furry, yellow-green, paw-like leaves

Echeveria: pale, matte, pink-tinted foliage

DESIGNING WITH
SCALE

For a display to work well it needs to suit the space in which it is placed. A tray of small plants can have as much impact as a single large plant, so long as their size is proportionate to the location and to one another.

SMALL IS BEAUTIFUL

While mini cacti and succulents look cute up close, they can easily lose their impact from a distance. For maximum impact, quantity is key. Grouping plants together creates a single focal point that attracts attention, especially when placed on a tray to define and unify the display. Choose a variety of different plants to draw interest through the arrangement, and position them in a low area such as a coffee table, where they can easily be admired from above as well as from the side.

IN THE MIDDLE

Mid-sized plants work well in an open space such as a broad windowsill. A multi-level display adds vertical interest, especially when using trailing plants to draw the eye down to the lower levels. Focus on a few similar features to tie the display together. In the display above, for instance, the trailing stems of the *Rhipsalis baccifera* mirror the wild, spiky outline of the *Euphorbia tirucalli* below.

MAKE A STATEMENT

A large mature plant standing alone can take on a sculptural presence, as if it were a work of living art. Celebrate this by displaying it as a single statement piece in a stand-out container, in a part of the room where it can really "own" the space around it and draw the eye towards it.

DESIGNING WITH
COLOUR

There's a range of different-coloured cacti and succulents to design with. Sticking with a single, harmonious palette (see below right) is the easiest way to build a bold arrangement that suits your living space. Working with a mix of contrasting colours is trickier, but if you can balance a variety of different shades without the display looking random, the result will look especially striking.

UNDERSTANDING COLOUR

Use the colour wheel below to identify the palette(s) that you want to incorporate in your display. Limiting yourself to adjacent tones (such as the warm shades on the right of the wheel) will create a harmonious palette; colours from opposite sides of the wheel will contrast with one another. A few variegated (two-tone) plants can add further interest to a display.

Cooler shades: blues, deep greens, purples

Warm shades: pinks, reds, oranges

Bright vivid greens

Variegated (two-tone)

REFRESHING GREENS

It may be the most common colour in the foliage spectrum, but a green palette is anything but boring. Combine vibrant green plants, such as *Crassula ovata* 'Hobbit' and *Cotyledon tomentosa*, with darker, more muted cacti to create a display that is refreshing and restful on the eye, while still feeling full of life.

"Limit yourself to a harmonious colour palette to create a display that looks deliberately designed and curated."

CONTRASTING PALETTE

An effective display of colour contrast needs to look deliberately curated, or else it will just appear random and disordered. This group evenly balances warm, cool, and green notes, with each plant and pot adding a vibrant pop of colour that draws the eye while never overwhelming the rest of the display.

WARM TONES

Any group of warm-coloured plants immediately provides an earthy, rustic effect. Red-spined cacti and yellow-tinted succulent foliage subtly evoke a desert or southern Mediterranean landscape. Try using a selection of red and terracotta pots to further emphasise this palette choice.

COOL AND CRISP

Blue- and purple-coloured succulents often appear quite pale and silvery, owing to the delicate powdery "bloom" that covers their foliage. To strengthen the impact of a cool-coloured display, the arrangement above includes a couple of brighter, pink–purple echeverias, and some deep blue containers.

DESIGNING WITH
TEXTURE

While it may seem more subtle than size or colour, texture can add an almost multisensory dimension to cactus and succulent displays. While you shouldn't actually touch a spiny cactus or disturb the bloom of a smooth, matte succulent leaf, these characteristics spark curiousity and draw the eye. Try grouping similarly textured plants (see below), or mix and match a few contrasting textures (see opposite) to emphasize their individuality.

UNDERSTANDING TEXTURE

The cuttings below demonstrate the wide range of textures different cacti and succulents can bring to an arrangement. The examples here range from smooth (top row) to rough and spiky specimens (bottom row), with glossier cuttings on the left leading to matte examples on the right.

Glossy foliage

Matte foliage

Smooth foliage

Spiny foliage

Furry foliage

SMOOTH AND NEAT

Whether glossy or matte, the smooth-textured foliage typical of many succulents can lend a clean silhouette to a display. Introduce other contrasting elements, such as colour and shape, to maximise visual interest.

FURRY FOLIAGE

Plants with a hairy or furry appearance can seem almost ethereal, especially when grouped together. When designing a furry display, less is definitely more; too many specimens will make the group seem untidy or wild. Limit yourself to a few distinct-looking plants to maximize their impact.

CONTRAST OF TEXTURE

In mixed-texture display, light will be reflected slightly differently by individual plants, giving each specimen a unique presence in the group. To unify them, find a few common features. For example, the plants above all share the same green colour palette, while the smooth pots emphasize their contrasting textures.

SPINY SPECIMENS

The eye-catching impact of cacti and euphorbia with huge, almost exaggerated spines is hard to beat. With so many spiny specimens available, feel free to play around with size and shape; a mix of columnar and globular cacti will emphasize the harmony of the plants' dramatic, dangerous texture.

CHOOSING
CONTAINERS

A great plant arrangement is as much about your choice of pots as it is about your choice of plants. By keeping your plants potted up in plastic containers with good drainage holes (see p193), you can easily swap one decorative outer pot (known as a "sleeve") for another until you find which one suits it best. That might mean a container that harmonizes (or contrasts) with the plant's colour or texture, one that gives the plant a unique outline, or another quality entirely. Keep swapping between pots until you find your perfect match.

THE PERFECT MATCH

Successfully pairing plants with pots takes practice, as you learn what works and what doesn't. The right container needs to not only highlight your plant's best characteristics (see pp10–11), but also suit your living space and complement the other pots and plants within a group display.

1

2

The *Agave*'s dramatic foliage is emphasized by the bold, geometric pot

The *Sedum*'s diminutive size is offset by a vividly patterned, eye-catching pot

3

ONE PLANT, THREE POTS

As the paddle kalanchoe on the left shows, the choice of container completely changes the plant's visual impact:

1 The tall, smooth pot gives the plant an architectural outline, while the pale colour sets off the vivid variegated (two-tone) leaves.

2 A textured pot contrasts with the smooth foliage, while the terracotta picks up on the plant's warm red tones.

3 A metallic pot enhances the kalanchoe's strange, almost alien appearance.

The *Opuntia*'s round outline and spiny texture contrasts with the smooth, straight-sided pot, while its bright green colour harmonizes with the light green pot

The spiny *Euphorbia* finds an almost comical textural contrast in a soft fabric pot sleeve

The flowering *Echeveria* makes a statement in a stripy monochrome pot

The *Kalanchoe*'s colourful foliage clashes perfectly with the bright, solid blue pot

The tips of this *Echeveria* harmonize with this bright orange pot

DESIGNING WITH
CONTAINERS

You can create some exciting displays by giving the containers a starring role too, rather than using them simply to play a supporting role. Here are a few examples of what you can do to make a bold statement with your choice of pots.

CACTUS THEATRE

This is a scaled-down version of a classic cactus display method. Here, a multilevel arrangement showcasing a variety of cacti and cacti-like euphorbias are all presented in identical terracotta pots. The symmetry of the pots, and their direct colour contrast with the plants' foliage, creates a striking overall impression that unifies the whole while accentuating the unique qualities of each cactus.

A ROW OF THREE

Repetition of three is a tried and tested design device, and can make an especially effective impression when a trio of neat, geometrical pots are brought together in a row. The group above features three rosette-shaped plants displayed in cube-shaped containers, resulting in a smart, symmetrical display.

UPCYCLED CONTAINERS

Brand-new, purpose-made plant pots can look stunning, but don't be afraid to be a bit braver with your container choices. Pre-loved antique terracotta pots, for instance, can add a rustic charm to a display. Repurposed household items and charity-shop finds can be transformed into quirky cactus and succulent containers. Mugs and bowls make excellent outer sleeves, while colanders (see right) can be planted into directly, since their holes conveniently offer built-in drainage.

BRINGING IT ALL
TOGETHER

The more you design cacti and
succulent displays, the more bold
and creative your arrangements
will become. Keep in mind how to
work with size, colour, and texture,
and select containers that will
complement your plants and your
living space. Your home will soon
become a lush indoor oasis.

The clean
architectural
outlines of these
different-sized
African spear plants
define the space
beside the sofa

Positioning plants in front of a mirror creates the illusion of an even larger display, while the reflection provides an all-round view

The combination of two tall succulents with a trailing *Rhipsalis* fills an empty corner of the room

A large *Echinocactus* is grouped with a varied selection of smaller cacti and *Euphorbia* in warm-toned terracotta pots, creating a statement across the coffee table

PLANT
PROJECTS

BROKEN POT PLANTER

Give new life to broken clay plant pots by reworking them into a tiered display for eye-catching succulents. The open side of one big pot can make a window for smaller broken pot pieces and, with careful planting, will create an impressive layered effect. Take care when handling broken pots as the edges may be sharp.

WHAT YOU WILL NEED

PLANTS
- Selection of succulent plants of differing sizes, colours, and textures, such as aeoniums, crassulas, sedums, and echeverias

OTHER MATERIALS
- One large broken clay pot with a drainage hole in the base, with matching saucer
- Cactus compost
- 2–3 smaller clay pots, broken or whole
- A selection of broken pot pieces
- Small pebbles

TOOLS
- Trowel
- Dibber
- Soft-bristled paintbrush, for dusting
- Spoon
- Watering can with narrow spout

1 Fill one-third of the large pot with compost and firm it down. Arrange the smaller pots within the larger pot at irregular angles, filling them with compost as you go.

2 Fill the spaces around the smaller pots with compost. Use broken pot pieces to wedge everything in place, if necessary. Make sure that the composition leaves plenty of exposed compost and space for planting.

3 Remove the first plant from its pot and gently loosen the roots. Make a hole in the compost the same size as the root ball and place the plant in it. Use the dibber to firm the compost around the base of the plant.

4 Repeat this process with the smaller plants, allowing some space between them for growth. If necessary, use broken pot pieces to support the plants.

5 Fill narrower spaces by gently prizing apart the roots of compact plants to make 2-3 smaller plants. Carefully bed these plants into the gaps.

6 When you are happy with the arrangement, brush any remaining compost from the surface of the plants and cover any exposed compost with the small pebbles.

HOW TO MAINTAIN

TEMPERATURE 10-25°C (50-77°F)
LIGHT Filtered sun
HUMIDITY Low

WATERING Use a watering can with a narrow spout to water around the plants, ensuring that all the separate areas receive enough water. Wait until the compost has dried out completely before watering again.

MAINTENANCE AND CARE Stand in bright indirect light, turning the display occasionally to ensure all the plants receive enough sun.

HANGING BASKET

Add vertical interest to your room with a hanging succulent planter. Trailing cacti such as *Rhipsalis* and *Epiphyllum* are epiphytic, meaning that they grow naturally from the surface of trees in the canopy of the rainforest. Suspended from a moss-lined basket, with some plants emerging from holes in the basket's sides, these plants will drape beautifully.

WHAT YOU WILL NEED

PLANTS
- 3 or 5 trailing cacti and succulents, such as ceropegias, epiphyllums, and rhipsalis

OTHER MATERIALS
- 2m (6½ft) strong twine or rope
- Wire basket
- Sheet of sphagnum moss, around 1.5cm (½in) thick
- Orchid compost (see p192)

TOOLS
- Trowel
- Wire cutters
- Scissors
- Small sharp knife
- Watering can with narrow spout
- Tray, for watering

1 Cut the twine into four equal lengths around 50cm (1½ft) long. Knot the first piece around the edge of the basket so that it has two tails of equal length. Repeat with the other pieces at equal points around the basket.

2 Place the spaghnum moss around the inside and on the bottom of the basket. This will provide a lining for the compost, so it is important to ensure that there are no gaps.

3 Add compost to the moss-lined basket until it is three-quarters full. Gather the pieces of string above the frame and knot them together to make a secure loop.

4 Using the wire cutters, make 2–3 evenly distributed holes in the side of the basket frame to create space to display some of your trailing plants.

5 Select your first plant. Compress its root ball in your fingers and carefully push it into one of the holes and through the moss. Repeat to fill the remaining holes.

6 Plant up the top of the basket with any remaining cacti and succulents, firming the compost around each plant so that they sit snugly in place.

HOW TO MAINTAIN

TEMPERATURE 10–25°C (50–77°F)
LIGHT Light shade
HUMIDITY Medium

WATERING Lift the basket to judge if it needs water; the lighter the basket, the drier the soil. The size of the basket is directly related to the amount of water your hanging plants can retain, meaning that a smaller basket will need to be watered more often than a larger one. Place a tray under the basket before watering to catch the drips, then use a watering can to soak any exposed compost. Mist the basket occasionally, as these plants prefer humid conditions.

MAINTENANCE AND CARE Hang the basket in a bright area out of direct sun.

SAND TERRARIUM

This terrarium provides the perfect environment for an assortment of desert-loving cacti and succulents to grow together. The plants will seem at home nestled in the layered sand, which is cleverly kept separate from the cactus compost by placing a second smaller container within the outer vase.

WHAT YOU WILL NEED

PLANTS
- A selection of desert-loving cacti and succulents with a variety of shapes and textures

OTHER MATERIALS
- Small pebbles or gravel
- 17cm (7in) glass vase
- Cactus compost
- 20cm (8in) glass vase
- Decorative sand in 2-3 contrasting colours

TOOLS
- Trowel
- Dibber
- Cactus gloves
- Piece of stiff card or paper
- Small paintbrush, for dusting
- Watering can with narrow spout
- Moisture metre

1 Pour a 5cm (2in) layer of small pebbles or gravel into the smaller vase, then fill it almost to the top with the compost.

2 Choose an eye-catching focal plant. Remove the plant from its pot and gently loosen the roots. Using the dibber, make a hole in the compost large enough to fit the plant's root ball. Place the plant in the hole.

3 Firm the compost around the plant with the dibber. Repeat with the remaining plants, taking care and wearing gloves when handling the cacti.

4 Pour a layer of pebbles or gravel into the larger vase. Place the planted vase inside the larger vase, ensuring that the rims of the two vases are level with each other.

5 Use the stiff card to funnel the first layer of sand between the two vases, allowing it to settle in uneven waves. Continue to layer different colours of sand until the space is filled and the inner vase is entirely hidden.

6 Brush off any compost or sand from the plants' foliage before displaying the terrarium.

HOW TO MAINTAIN

TEMPERATURE 10–25°C (50–77°F)
LIGHT Filtered sun
HUMIDITY Low

WATERING Use a narrow-spouted watering can to pour a small amount of water onto the compost around the plants. As this terrarium does not have drainage holes, take extra care to avoid overwatering your plants. You may wish to insert a moisture metre into the soil now and then to help you judge if you are using the correct amount of water; cacti and succulents prefer to be kept in soil at the red end of the metre.

MAINTENANCE AND CARE Choose a bright and sunny spot for the terrarium. Move the display a little away from the window in summer months, as direct light may scorch the plants.

SUCCULENT GLOBE

Made with two compost-filled hanging-basket frames, this living globe seems to defy gravity. Low-growing, rosette-shaped plants work best for this project, as they help maintain the display's spherical outline, but you could also try adding a few trailing plants near the bottom of the globe to create a living waterfall effect.

WHAT YOU WILL NEED

PLANTS
- A selection of small succulents, such as echeverias and sempervivums
- 2-3 trailing plants, such as *Curio rowleyanus* (optional)
- Decorative moss

OTHER MATERIALS
- 2 coir fibre liners
- 2 x 25cm (10in) hemispherical wire hanging baskets
- Cactus compost
- Florist's wire
- Strong cord, twine, or chain
- Florist's pins

EQUIPMENT
- Baking sheet or wooden board
- Wire cutters
- Sharp scissors
- Dibber (optional)
- Deep tray
- Plastic funnel, for watering
- Jug

1 Place a coir fibre liner inside each basket. Fill with compost up to the top of the baskets. Pack it in as tightly as possible, because any air pockets that remain could cause the coir fibre to sag later.

2 Hold the baking sheet against the top of one of the baskets. Quickly and carefully flip the basket and sheet over, and place them directly on top of the other basket. Ease out the sheet, taking care not to let any compost leak.

3 Use florist's wire to attach the outer edges of the baskets to each other at regular intervals. They should now form a secure "globe". Loop a piece of strong cord around one of the baskets' bars, ready to hang up the globe later.

4 At the opposite side of the globe to the cord, cut a small hole in the coir liner and tease it open. Remove the first plant from its pot and gently shake away the excess compost. Squeeze the root ball in your hand and insert it into the hole.

5 Firm the coir fibre back around the plant, then secure it with a florist's pin. Repeat steps 4–5 with the remaining plants, positioning them evenly around the globe with enough room between them to allow for growth.

6 When most of the globe is covered, invert it and hang it up from a secure point. Carefully plant up any empty areas on what was the underside. Once the whole globe is covered with plants, pin decorative moss onto any exposed areas of coir.

HOW TO MAINTAIN

TEMPERATURE 10–25°C (50–77°F)
LIGHT Full sun; some shade in summer
HUMIDITY Low

WATERING Place a deep tray under the hanging globe to catch any drips. Standing on a stepladder if necessary, carefully insert a funnel into the coir lining at the top of the globe and pour water into the funnel to saturate the compost within. Let all excess water to drain away before removing the tray. Allow the compost to dry out fully in between waterings; you will be able to tell from the weight of the globe when it needs to be watered again.

MAINTENANCE AND CARE Display the globe in bright, indirect light, turning it in between waterings to ensure all the plants get plenty of sun. The globe will be heavy, especially after watering, so make sure to hang it from a secure point able to take the full weight of the display when saturated.

INDOOR WINDOW BOX

An indoor window box lets you take advantage of the brightest location in your home and offers the ideal conditions for your cacti and succulents to grow. By building your own box out of timber or reclaimed wood, you can make a display that will perfectly fill the length of your windowsill.

WHAT YOU WILL NEED

PLANTS
- Selection of mid-sized cacti and succulents

OTHER MATERIALS
- New or reclaimed timber boards
- Screws or nails
- Wood paint or stain (optional)
- Plastic sheeting
- 4mm grit or fine gravel
- Cactus compost
- Small pebbles

TOOLS
- Tape measure
- Saw
- Screwdriver or hammer
- Large paintbrush, for painting
- Staple gun
- Trowel
- Dibber
- Cactus gloves
- Spoon
- Soft-bristled paintbrush, for dusting
- Watering can with narrow spout

1 Measure the length of your chosen windowsill (see How to Maintain, opposite). Saw 3 equal lengths of timber slightly smaller than the sill (to form the base and sides), followed by 2 short lengths for the ends. Screw or hammer the sides to the base, then secure the end pieces in place.

2 If you wish, apply 1–2 coats of wood paint or stain to the outside of the box, following the instructions provided on the tin. Allow to dry completely.

3 When the box is fully dry, line the inside with plastic sheeting and staple it securely in place, to make it as watertight as possible.

4 Pour a layer of 4mm grit, about 2cm (¾in) deep, into the bottom of the box. Then fill it with a loose layer of cactus compost until it reaches up to 5cm (2in) from the top.

5 Select the first plant. Use the dibber to make a hole in the compost large enough to fit the plant's root ball. Wearing cactus gloves, remove the plant from its pot and loosen its roots, then gently place it into the hole. Firm down the compost around the plant.

6 Repeat with the remaining plants, placing them at regular intervals along the box. Leave some space between the plants to allow for growth and good air circulation, which reduces the risk of rot.

HOW TO MAINTAIN

TEMPERATURE 10–25°C (50–77°F)
LIGHT Filtered sun
HUMIDITY Low

WATERING Using a watering can with a narrow spout, water around the plants when the compost is completely dry. Take care not to overwater. Reduce watering between late autumn and early spring.

MAINTENANCE AND CARE Choose a windowsill that receives filtered or indirect sunlight; direct sunlight could scorch the plants in summer. Avoid draughty windowsills too, as well as those with radiators beneath them, as the heat may dry out the plants.

7 Once all the plants are in place, place decorative gravel on top of the compost, then gently brush off any compost with a soft-bristled paintbrush.

HYPERTUFA POT

Combining just three ingredients with water creates hypertufa, a clay-like mixture that can be used to make your own plant pot. Not only do hypertufa pots make great statement containers (see pp18–19), but they are also porous and lightweight, making them ideal for planting up desert cacti and succulents. This project takes around a month to complete, but it's well worth the wait.

WHAT YOU WILL NEED

MATERIALS
- Portland cement
- Coir fibre
- Perlite or vermiculite

TOOLS
- Cardboard or plastic sheeting, to protect surfaces (optional)
- Rubber gloves
- Bucket, for mixing
- Cooking oil spray
- 2 plastic containers, 1 larger than the other, to be used as moulds
- Rubber mallet
- Large plastic bag
- Stiff wire brush
- Plastic tray

1 Cover your work surface. In a bucket, combine equal parts cement, coir fibre, and perlite, bearing in mind the size of the pot you will be making. Put on rubber gloves, then stir the mixture together while gradually adding 1 part water until it resembles thick porridge. Allow to sit for 5–10 minutes.

2 Spray the inside of the larger container and the outside of the smaller container with oil. Press some of the mixture into the bottom of the larger container, firming it down into the corners. Gradually add more mixture, applying a thick, even layer to the sides.

3 Insert the smaller container into the mixture-lined larger container, pressing it firmly onto the bottom and around the sides. Continue packing more mixture between the containers until it feels firm. Ensure that at least 2.5cm (1in) of plastic remains exposed at the top of each container.

4 Tap around the outside of the container with a rubber mallet to encourage any large bubbles to move to the surface. Use your fingers to smooth any lumps around the top edge. Place inside a large plastic bag, seal it securely, then leave to dry and harden for 24–36 hours.

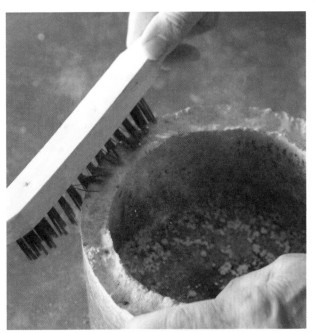

5 Remove the pot from the bag. Scratch the exposed rim with a fingernail to see if it has hardened. If it is still soft, leave it for a few more hours before retesting. When only a screwdriver can scratch the surface, remove the containers. If they are hard to move, gently tap the sides with the mallet to loosen them.

6 Leave in a dry place for 2-3 weeks to finish drying. The pot will turn light gray and will feel significantly lighter. Scrub the top edge of the pot with a wire brush to smooth away any sharp edges. Do not scrub too much; the pot should still look rustic.

7 Place the pot in a plastic tray then fill both with water. Leave to soak for a day, then pour away the water and repeat. This will leach away any alkaline compounds in the hypertufa mixture that could otherwise cause your plants to suffer. After 10 days, pour away the water and leave to dry thoroughly. The pot is now ready to be planted up.

HOW TO MAINTAIN

MAINTENANCE AND CARE To avoid scratches to floors and furniture, you may wish to glue felt to the underside of the pot. As hypertufa is relatively porous, plants can be potted up directly into the pot, without the need for a plastic container. However, as always, you should still take care to avoid overwatering.

BARK SUCCULENT PLANTER

Create a contrast of colour and texture by planting a varied collection of succulents into a piece of bark or driftwood. Low-growing succulents are perfect for this project as they are shallow-rooted and therefore require little planting space. If using ocean driftwood, soak it in soapy water for 2 weeks to desalinate it and make it safe for planting.

WHAT YOU WILL NEED

PLANTS
- A selection of low-growing succulents of different shapes, colours, and textures, such as sempervivums and echeverias

OTHER MATERIALS
- Piece of freestanding bark or desalinated driftwood
- Sphagnum moss
- Cactus compost

TOOLS
- Power drill with spade bit (optional)
- Stiff-bristled paintbrush
- Florist's wire
- Wire cutters
- Soft-bristled paintbrush, for dusting
- Spoon
- Watering can with narrow spout

1 Use a power drill fitted with a spade bit to create extra planting holes along the piece of wood if needed. Carefully remove unwanted dirt and debris from the surface of the wood with a stiff-bristled paintbrush.

2 Line the crevices and holes in the base of the bark with a small amount of sphagnum moss, then top with compost.

3 Loosen the roots of the first plant. Push it firmly into the compost, right up alongside the edge of one of the planting holes, making sure that the roots are fully buried in the compost.

4 Repeat step 3 with the remaining plants, nestling them quite tightly together to mimic the way they would grow naturally. Pack moss around any exposed compost to hold the plants firmly in place.

5 If the planting hole is quite shallow, secure the plants and moss with florist's wire until the roots take hold.

6 Use the soft-bristled paintbrush to gently brush off any loose compost or moss from the plants.

HOW TO MAINTAIN

TEMPERATURE 10-25°C (50-77°F)
LIGHT Filtered sun
HUMIDITY Low

WATERING Water around the base of the plants to encourage the roots to grow and spread, enabling the plants to settle in. Allow the compost to dry out fully before watering again. Reduce watering in the winter months.

MAINTENANCE AND CARE Place the display in bright, filtered light. If one of the plants eventually outgrows the bark, you can divide it: gently remove it from the compost and separate it into 2-3 smaller pieces. Replant one of the pieces in the vacant space and plant the remaining piece(s) in another pot.

INDOOR ROCKERY

In their native South Africa, *Lithops* (also known as living stones) avoid being eaten by camouflaging themselves to look like the surrounding rocks. Make the most of this feature by nestling them with other low-growing succulents amongst a mini-landscape of rocks and pebbles. As these plants prefer their roots to be restricted, keep them in their individual pots when you plant them.

WHAT YOU WILL NEED

PLANTS
- Pebble-like plants such as lithops and pachyphytums

OTHER MATERIALS
- 4mm grit or fine gravel
- Shallow decorative container, preferably with drainage holes
- Cactus compost
- Decorative rocks and pebbles

TOOLS
- Spoons or small trowels
- Dibber
- Soft-bristled paintbrush, for dusting
- Watering can with narrow spout

1 Pour a layer of gravel, about 2.5cm (1in) deep, into the bottom of the container. Cover the gravel with an even layer of compost of a similar thickness.

2 Arrange the plants (still in their original plastic pots) on top of the compost. Leave some space between the plants for the rocks and stones to be added later.

3 Fill in the space between the plastic pots with the compost until the pot rims are no longer visible. Firm the compost down with a spoon or dibber.

4 Cover the surface of the compost with a mix of decorative rocks and pebbles until the compost is no longer visible.

5 Use a small paintbrush to gently remove any stray compost from the plants.

HOW TO MAINTAIN

TEMPERATURE 5–25°C (41–77°F)
LIGHT Full sun; some shade in summer
HUMIDITY Low

WATERING From spring to early autumn, after the lithops' old leaves have withered, water when the top of the compost is dry. From late autumn to late winter, keep the compost almost dry, watering around the pachyphytum occasionally to prevent their leaves from shrivelling. Take care not to overwater; the plants may rot in wet compost, and the lithops could split open.

MAINTENANCE AND CARE Place the rockery in a bright spot near a window. Provide light shade in midsummer to avoid scorching the plants.

POTTED PLANT WREATH

An assortment of new and recycled terracotta pots in different sizes not only put an eye-catching spin on a classic wreath, but also allow you to display living plants rather than cuttings. The plants in this arrangement create a warm colour palette to match the pots (see pp14–15), but you could also try combining white pots with blue-tinted plants for a more cool look.

WHAT YOU WILL NEED

PLANTS
- A selection of low-growing succulents, such as crassulas, echeverias, sedums, and sempervivums
- Decorative moss

OTHER MATERIALS
- Florist's wire
- A selection of 6cm (2½in) and 12cm (5in) terracotta pots with drainage holes
- Willow or wire wreath frame
- Cactus compost
- Strong twine or string

TOOLS
- Wire cutters
- Hot glue gun
- Spoon or small trowel
- Watering can with narrow spout
- Wide tray, for watering

1 Run a length of florist's wire through the drainage hole of one of the larger pots. Bring the ends of the wire together on the outside of the pot and twist together, as shown.

2 Position the pot at an angle beside the wreath frame. Wrap the wire ends around the frame and twist to secure. Repeat this process for the remaining large pots, spacing them equally around the frame.

3 Add the smaller pots to the frame using the method described in steps 1–2, filling in the gaps between the larger pots, alternating the angles of the pots as you go.

4 Once you are happy with the overall composition of the pots on the frame, secure them in place with a hot glue gun. Add compost to the base of each pot.

5 Add a plant to each pot, firming it down into the compost. If the plant will be upside-down once the wreath is hung up, run 1–2 pieces of wire across the lip of the pot between the compost and the plant's foliage and secure it to the frame.

6 Pack some moss around the surface of the compost and around the frame, securing it discreetly in place with florist's wire.

7 Leave the wreath to lie flat for up to 1 month to allow the plants to settle into their pots. To hang the wreath up, loop a piece of strong twine around the frame and secure with a firm knot.

HOW TO MAINTAIN

TEMPERATURE 5–25°C (41–77°F)
LIGHT Filtered sun
HUMIDITY Low

WATERING Place the wreath flat in a wide tray, then water each of the plants in turn using a watering can with a narrow spout. Leave the wreath lying down to drain before re-hanging. Allow the compost in the pots to dry out completely between waterings.

MAINTAINENCE AND CARE Display the wreath in bright indirect light. If any of the succulents start to outgrow their pots, take the wreath down and replant the pot with a new, small plant.

FLOATING TERRARIUM GARDEN

Maximize your space by displaying your own hanging terrarium garden across a window that receives plenty of bright, filtered light. Globe terrariums with large openings are best for this project, as they will provide the plants with plenty of air circulation.

WHAT YOU WILL NEED

PLANTS
- A selection of small and low-growing cacti and succulents, such as echeverias, crassulas, kalanchoes, and mammillarias

OTHER MATERIALS
- Wooden branch or pole (optional)
- 2 curtain brackets (optional)
- Screws (optional)
- 4mm grit or gravel
- A selection of small- and medium-sized hanging globe terrariums
- Cactus compost
- Small pebbles
- Twine or clear plastic wire

TOOLS
- Screwdriver (optional)
- Spirit level (optional)
- Spoon or small trowel
- Dibber
- Watering can with narrow spout

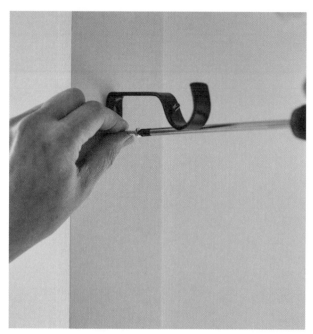

1 If you are putting up a new branch or pole, position a curtain bracket to one side of your chosen window and screw it in place. Repeat on the other side of the window, ensuring the brackets are level, then add the branch or pole.

2 Select your first terrarium. Spoon a layer of grit or gravel into the bottom. Top with a loose layer of compost approximately 2.5cm (1in) deep.

3 Remove your first plant from its pot and gently loosen the roots. Make a hole in the compost at the back of the terrarium and place the plant in it. Use a dibber to gently firm the compost around the base of the plant.

4 Repeat the process with 1–2 additional plants, ensuring that there is sufficient space between them for air circulation and growth. Place any trailing plants nearest the front, so that the stems can emerge from the opening.

5 Scatter decorative pebbles on top of any exposed compost. Repeat steps 2-5 for the remaining terrariums.

6 Thread a piece of twine through each terrarium's loop. Tie the ends securely around the loops at the top of the branch or pole. Vary the length of each piece of twine so that the terrariums "float" at different levels across the window.

HOW TO MAINTAIN

TEMPERATURE 8-25°C (46-77°F)
LIGHT Filtered sun
HUMIDITY Low

WATERING Use a watering can with a narrow spout to water the plants. Because they lack drainage and are partially covered, plants displayed in terraria retain moisture for longer than usual, making them more susceptible to overwatering and rot. Therefore, take care to water them only very occasionally, once the compost has completely dried out.

MAINTENANCE AND CARE These terrariums are best displayed beside a window that receives filtered light for a few hours a day; too much bright, full sunlight could scorch the plants through the terrarium glass.

PLANTED CANDLE HOLDER

Simple to make, this beautiful table centrepiece looks great all year round. If you like, you can easily switch the candle for one of a different colour to match the season or change the mood. Choose a slow-burning, dripless candle that will sit at least 10cm (4in) above the plants to avoid dripping hot wax onto the foliage.

WHAT YOU WILL NEED

PLANTS

- A selection of low growing succulents, such as sedums, echeverias, and crassulas
- A trailing plant, such as *Curio rowleyanus*
- Decorative moss

OTHER MATERIALS

- Fine-grade gravel
- Terracotta pot, 20cm (8in) wide
- Terracotta pot, 12cm (5in) wide
- Cactus compost
- 16cm (6in) pillar candle, dripless if possible

TOOLS

- Trowel
- Dibber
- Spoon
- Soft-bristled paintbrush, for dusting
- Watering can with narrow spout

1 Pour a layer of gravel into the bottom of the larger pot. Place the smaller pot into the centre of the larger one, ensuring that the outer rims of both pots are level.

2 Fill the space between the two pots with compost, but leave a 2cm (1in) gap at the top. Pack the compost down firmly to secure the small pot in the centre.

3 Remove the first plant from its pot and gently loosen its roots. Using the dibber, make a hole in the compost and place the plant in it, firmly packing down the compost around the plant.

4 Repeat step 3 with the remaining plants. As the area between the two pots is quite narrow, you may need to divide the plants following the instructions on p29.

5 Place the candle in the smaller pot. Pack moss around the candle to secure it in place. Use the paintbrush to remove any remaining moss or debris from the plants.

HOW TO MAINTAIN

TEMPERATURE 10–25°C (50–77°F)
LIGHT Filtered sun
HUMIDITY Low

WATERING Use a watering can with a narrow spout to direct the water onto the compost between the two pots. The gravel in the pot and hole at the base will stop the plants becoming waterlogged. Allow the compost to dry out fully before watering again.

MAINTENANCE AND CARE Keep in bright, indirect light. When the candle has burned low, replace it with a new one, packing it in place with fresh moss.

LEAF PROPAGATION DISPLAY

Leaf propagation (see pp200–01) is one of the simplest ways to expand your plant collection. While you wait for your new plants to grow, create a work of living art by arranging your leaves in an eye-catching design. It's best to try this project in the spring or summer when the leaves will propagate more readily.

WHAT YOU WILL NEED

PLANTS
- A variety of succulents with leaves of different sizes and colours, such as echeverias, sedums, and crassulas

OTHER MATERIALS
- 4mm grit or gravel
- Wide and shallow decorative dish, ideally with drainage holes
- Cactus compost

TOOLS
- Shallow dishes, for drying
- Trowel
- Tray, for sorting
- Mister or watering can with rose attachment

1 Remove the leaves from the succulents, using the method described on p201. Make sure to remove the whole leaf as the young plant will sprout from the base.

2 Put the leaves in shallow dishes and set aside in a dry place out of direct sunlight for a few days to allow each leaf base to callus over.

3 Pour a layer of gravel, about 2.5cm (1in) deep, into the bottom of the decorative dish. Cover the gravel with an even layer of cactus compost of the same thickness.

4 Arrange the leaves on a tray so that you can clearly group them together, sorting them by size and colour. Starting with the largest leaves, place them around the edge of the dish, ensuring that the callused bases only rest on surface of the compost (do not bury them).

5 Continue to arrange the leaves in rings around the dish. Experiment with different repeating patterns of colour and leaf type, but try to alternate the direction of the leaves, so that no two leaf bases are directly beside one another; this will maximize the amount of rooting space each leaf will have.

6 If you wish, finish the design by inserting a stem cutting from one of the stripped plants (see p203) into the centre. As with the leaves, ensure that the stem is callused over, then gently insert it into the exposed compost.

HOW TO MAINTAIN

TEMPERATURE 10–25°C (50–77°F)
LIGHT Filtered sun
HUMIDITY Low

WATERING Do not water the display for a few weeks, until roots begin to form. Once the leaves begin to propagate, occasionally mist the display or lightly water it using a watering can with a rose attachment.

MAINTAIN Place the dish in a bright, dry spot out of direct sunlight. This project mimics step 1 of the leaf propagation process on pp200–01, with the compost-filled dish standing in as a decorative alternative to placing the leaves on kitchen towel. Once the leaves begin to propagate, you can either pot them on in separate containers, or push them gently into the soil of the dish to continue growing. If any leaves dry up without propagating, remove them and replace them with fresh leaves.

PLANT PROFILES

Use this chapter to look up your plant's unique care needs, and explore the 200 plant profiles to find inspiration to expand your collection further. While cacti are technically succulents, for ease of use the chapter is divided into two sections: Cacti (see pp76–125) and Succulents (see pp126–81).

CACTI

The feature that distinguishes cacti from other succulents (see pp126–81) is the round, cushion-like areas on their stems, known as "areoles", from which spines can grow. They also almost exclusively hail from the Americas. Cacti can range from tiny spiky globe-shaped plants to elegant smooth-stemmed trailers, and can generally be grouped into two types: desert-dwelling specimens, which prefer low humidity and bright light conditions; and tropical types such as the Christmas cactus (see p120), which hail from rainforests and thrive in shadier spots with higher levels of humidity.

ACANTHOCEREUS

The distinctive upright or arching ribbed stems of *Acanthocereus* are covered with rows of vicious thorny spines. In summer, mature plants produce white or yellow flowers that open at night – in some species the blooms are also scented. The flowers are then followed by inedible red fruits. Only cultivars of *Acanthocereus tetragonus* are widely available as house plants, but since they can grow up to 1.8m (6ft) in height indoors, allow sufficient space to display their spiky, statuesque stems.

TEMPERATURE 10–30°C (50–86°F)

LIGHT Position in full sun, but provide some shade in summer.

WATERING During the spring and summer, water when the top 2cm (¾in) of compost is dry. In autumn, reduce watering. Keep plants dry in winter.

FEEDING Apply an all-purpose granular fertilizer in spring at half the dose recommended on the label.

COMPOST Plant in cactus compost, or a 50:50 mix of loam-based (John Innes No. 2) compost and 4mm grit.

FLOWERING Flowers appear only on mature plants and rarely form on house plants.

PROPAGATION Sow seed or take offsets.

COMMON PROBLEMS These plants are prone to rotting in wet compost. Check regularly for mealybugs, scale insect, and spider mites.

ACANTHOCEREUS TETRAGONUS 'FAIRY CASTLES'
syn. *Cereus tetragonus* 'Fairy Castles'
Fairy-castle cactus

One of the most popular cultivars of *Acanthocereus tetragonus*, the fairy-castle cactus produces bright green ribbed stems that soon form small clusters. The ribs are edged with woolly clusters of short, creamy-white bristles, which produce a decorative striped pattern down the stems. The nocturnal white or yellow flowers are rarely produced on plants grown indoors, as this cactus needs to be large and mature to bloom.

HEIGHT AND SPREAD Up to 1m x 30cm (36 x 12in).

CARE NOTES See opposite.

CAUTION Wear cactus gloves when handling this plant.

ARIOCARPUS

An unusual cactus, many plants in the *Ariocarpus* group look like little green starfish and make a great contrast to a collection of round or column-shaped species. While most other cacti have "tubercules" in the form of raised bumps, on *Ariocarpus* they resemble triangular leaf-like sections. Only the seedlings have soft spines, which fall off as the plant matures, making this a good choice for homes with children or pets. The funnel-shaped flowers appear only when the plants are mature, so you may have to be patient. When they do arrive, the blooms develop from a woolly section at the top of the plant in autumn. They come in a range of colours, including white, yellow, pink, purple, and magenta.

TEMPERATURE -10–30°C (14–86°F); this plant will survive -10°C (14°F) if the soil is dry.

LIGHT Position in full sun, but provide some shade in summer.

WATERING During the spring and summer, water when the top 1cm (½in) of compost is dry. In autumn, reduce watering to once a month. Keep plants dry in winter.

FEEDING Apply a half-strength high-potash fertilizer fortnightly during late spring and summer.

COMPOST Plant in cactus compost, or a 50:50 mix of loam-based (John Innes No. 2) compost and 4mm grit.

FLOWERING Flowers only appear on mature plants; buy one in bloom to guarantee flowers the following year.

PROPAGATION Sow seed.

COMMON PROBLEMS These plants are prone to rotting in wet compost. Check regularly for mealybugs and spider mites.

ARIOCARPUS RETUSUS

syn. *Mammillaria areolosa;
Mammillaria prismatica*
Star rock; Cobbler's thumb

One of the most widely available *Ariocarpus*, the star rock produces a rosette of fat, triangular, blue-green or grey tubercules (leaf-like sections). These are arranged in a star shape, hence the name. The flowers appear in autumn and are white or pink. This *Ariocarpus* is very slow-growing and suitable only for those with the patience to watch it develop over many years.

HEIGHT AND SPREAD Up to 8 x 20cm (3 x 8in).

CARE NOTES See left.

ASTROPHYTUM

Admired for their round or columnar shape, patterned stems, and colourful flowers, these cacti are popular with keen collectors. The green or blue-green ribbed stems are, in some species, covered with tiny hairy scales that give them a silvery sheen. While many plants are spineless, others are armed with long or twisted spines. The daisy-like flowers, which can be white, yellow, pink, or red, appear in summer at the top of the plant and resemble pompoms on a cap.

TEMPERATURE -7–30°C (19–86°F); plants will tolerate short periods below freezing if the soil is dry.

LIGHT Position in full sun, but provide a little shade in summer.

WATERING During the spring and summer, water when the top 1cm (½in) of compost is dry. In autumn, reduce watering to once a month. Keep plants dry in winter. Provide good air circulation to reduce risk of rot.

FEEDING Apply a half-strength cactus fertilizer once a month during late spring and summer.

COMPOST Plant in cactus compost, or a 50:50 mix of loam-based (John Innes No. 2) compost and 4mm grit.

FLOWERING Flowers appear on mature plants; water regularly and provide a little fertilizer to guarantee blooms.

PROPAGATION Sow seed.

COMMON PROBLEMS These plants will rot in wet compost. Pests to look out for include mealybugs, scale insect, thrips, and spider mites.

ASTROPHYTUM CAPRICORNE AGM

syn. *Echinocactus capricornis*
Goat's horn cactus

The distinctive long curly spines of the goat's horn cactus are guaranteed to turn heads. While the ribbed stems of young plants are round, they soon form columns that can reach over 1m (3ft) in height, although restricting them to a pot usually keeps them smaller. The white woolly flecks on the stem also produce a decorative pattern, and the yellow and red flowers have a sweet fragrance.

HEIGHT AND SPREAD Up to 1m x 15cm (36 x 6in).

CARE NOTES See opposite.

ASTROPHYTUM MYRIOSTIGMA AGM

syn. *Cereus callicoche;*
Echinocactus myriostigma
Bishop's cap

The bishop's cap has broad ribs that look like the ceremonial head-dress of a bishop, after which this cactus is named. Young plants are round but soon grow into short columns, and their shimmering silver colour is produced by a coat of harmless hairy scales. Fragrant pale yellow flowers, sometimes reddish in the centre, appear intermittently from early spring to autumn.

HEIGHT AND SPREAD Up to 60 x 10cm (24 x 4in).

CARE NOTES See opposite.

ASTROPHYTUM ORNATUM AGM

syn. *Echinocactus ornatus*
Monk's hood cactus

One of the largest and easiest to grow of the *Astrophytum* species, the monk's hood cactus is globe-shaped when young but grows into a column as it matures. The stems are decorated with an unusual pattern of white scales, while the ribs are armed with clusters of brown or yellow spines. Yellow flowers appear in summer.

HEIGHT AND SPREAD Up to 30 x 15cm (12 x 6in).

CARE NOTES See opposite.

CAUTION Wear cactus gloves when handling this plant.

CEPHALOCEREUS

In their native Mexican habitat, these woolly-coated cacti can grow to a towering 12m (40ft). Restricted to a pot, however, this popular species maintains more manageable proportions. The stems form tall ribbed columns and some – including the popular *Cephalocereus senilis* – are covered with fine hairs that give them a distinctive cuddly appearance. Do not be fooled, though, as the long spines that protrude from the coat are sharp and dangerous. The flowers appear only on mature cacti and may never develop on those grown as house plants.

TEMPERATURE 5–30°C (41–86°F).

LIGHT Position in full sun.

WATERING During the spring and summer, water when the top 2cm (¾in) of compost is dry. In autumn, reduce watering. Keep plants dry in winter.

FEEDING Apply a slow-release general-purpose granular fertilizer in spring at half the dose recommended on the label.

COMPOST Plant in cactus compost, or a 50:50 mix of loam-based (John Innes No. 2) compost and 4mm grit.

FLOWERING Flowers will appear only on mature plants (around 10–20 years old).

PROPAGATION Sow seed or take stem cuttings.

COMMON PROBLEMS These plants will rot in wet compost. Pests to look out for include mealybugs, scale, and spider mites.

CEPHALOCEREUS SENILIS

syn. *Cephalophorus senilis;
Cereus senilis; Pilocereus senilis*
Old man cactus

The tall spiny stems of the old man cactus are wrapped in a yellowish-white hairy coat that resembles a scruffy beard – hence the name. This woolly covering may turn brown and become less dense on older plants. As it can grow quite big, display the plant's sculptural form on a wide sill next to a tall window or under a bright skylight. The trumpet-shaped blooms are whitish-yellow and open at night, but they are rarely seen on indoor plants and tend to develop only on mature cacti in the wild that are 6m (20ft) or more in height.

HEIGHT AND SPREAD Up to 1m x 8cm (3ft x 3in).

CARE NOTES See left.

CAUTION Wear cactus gloves when handling this plant.

CEREUS

These South American desert cacti are tall and tree-like in the wild, but smaller species and cultivars are grown indoors as house plants. However, even these may be too large for some homes, so check their heights and spreads before buying to ensure you can accommodate their tall, ribbed, spiny stems. This group of cacti are sometimes known as "night-blooming cereus" because their large, generally white, fragrant flowers open after dark. Plants may have pink, purple, or yellow blooms, and they usually appear in summer.

TEMPERATURE 5–30°C (41–86°F).

LIGHT Position in full sun, but provide some shade in summer.

WATERING During the spring and summer, water when the top 2cm (¾in) of compost is dry. In autumn, reduce watering to once a month. Keep plants dry in winter.

FEEDING Apply a half-strength high-potash fertilizer once a month during late spring and summer.

COMPOST Plant in cactus compost, or a 50:50 mix of loam-based (John Innes No. 2) compost and 4mm grit.

FLOWERING Flowers only appear on mature plants; buy one in bloom to guarantee flowers.

PROPAGATION Sow seed or take stem cuttings.

COMMON PROBLEMS These plants are prone to rotting in wet compost. Check regularly for mealybugs, scale insect, and spider mites.

CEREUS URUGUAYANUS 'MONSTROUS'

syn. *Cereus hildmannianus* subsp. *uruguayanus*
Spiny hedge cactus; Peruvian apple

If you have the space, the spiny hedge cactus will create a large sculptural feature in a bright sunny room. The blue-green cylindrical stems feature distinctive ribs covered with long golden or brown spines. Clusters of white summer flowers develop along the stems, and plants will flower and fruit when they are just 4 years old. In its native Uruguay, this cactus is grown for its edible fruits, which grow to the size of a goose egg.

HEIGHT AND SPREAD Up to 2m x 15cm (6ft 6in x 6in).

CARE NOTES See opposite.

CAUTION Wear cactus gloves when handling this plant.

CEREUS VALIDUS

syn. *Cereus forbesii;* *Cereus hankeanus*

This tall, sculptural *Cereus* is a cactus for the more experienced grower. Even in a pot, the blue-green cylindrical stems, armed with long spines, will eventually grow into a tree-like, branched plant. In spring to early summer, it produces large funnel-shaped white or pinkish-white flowers, followed by inedible red fruits.

HEIGHT AND SPREAD Each stem can grow up to 1.5m x 10cm (5ft x 4in).

CARE NOTES See opposite.

CAUTION Wear cactus gloves when handling this plant.

CEREUS VALIDUS 'SPIRALIS'

syn. *Cereus forbesii* 'Spiralis'
Spiralled cereus; Twisted cereus

Look no further than the spiralled cereus if you need a star performer for your cactus collection. The tall blue-green branched stems, which feature spiralling ribs edged with short spines, look like giant green corkscrews. This incredible cactus also produces a profusion of white and pink blooms in summer.

HEIGHT AND SPREAD Up to 1.5m x 60cm (5 x 2ft).

CARE NOTES See opposite.

CAUTION Wear cactus gloves when handling this plant.

CLEISTOCACTUS

Prickly desert-dwelling South American natives, *Cleistocactus* form either tall, slim, columnar structures or fountains of trailing stems, ideal for large hanging baskets. The cylindrical ribbed stems are covered with spines, which are soft in some species. Their long slim flowers, which look a little like tubes of lipstick, shoot out from the sides. The blooms can appear throughout the year on mature plants but are most prevalent in spring and summer. Some do not flower until they are 10-15 years old, so buy mature plants if this is a feature you want to enjoy.

TEMPERATURE 10-30°C (50-86°F)

LIGHT Position in full sun for most of the year, but provide some shade in summer.

WATERING During the spring and summer, water when the top 2cm (¾in) of compost is dry. In autumn, reduce watering to once a month. Keep the compost dry in winter.

FEEDING Apply a half-strength high-potash fertilizer fortnightly during late spring and summer.

COMPOST Plant in cactus compost, or a 50:50 mix of loam-based (John Innes No. 2) compost and 4mm grit.

FLOWERING Flowers appear on mature plants. Water regularly in spring and summer to encourage blooms to form.

PROPAGATION Sow seed or take stem cuttings.

COMMON PROBLEMS These plants will rot in wet compost. Pests to look out for include mealybugs and spider mites.

CLEISTOCACTUS COLADEMONONIS AGM

syn. *Cleistocactus winteri* subsp. *colademononis;* *Hildewintera colademononis;* *Winterocereus colademononis* Rat's tail; Monkey's tail

Resembling white furry octopus tentacles, the stems of this striking plant are a guaranteed talking point. The hairs are actually long soft spines growing on stems that can reach up to 2m (6ft 6in) in length. Bright red tubular flowers, up to 7.5cm (3in) long, appear along the stems in spring and sometimes at other times of the year. Display this stunning cactus in a large hanging basket where it will form an eye-catching feature in a sunny room.

HEIGHT & SPREAD Each stem grows up to 5cm x 2m (2in x 6ft 6in).

CARE NOTES See left.

CAUTION Plant is toxic if eaten.

CLEISTOCACTUS PARVIFLORUS

syn. *Cereus parviflorus*

One of the columnar species, *Cleistocactus parviflorus* produces towering, slim, ribbed stems up to 3cm (1½in) in diameter, covered with fine brown to greenish-yellow spines. The small tubular flowers are usually yellow, although some plants may produce red blooms.

HEIGHT & SPREAD Each stem grows up to 3m x 7cm (10ft x 3in).

CARE NOTES See left.

CAUTION Plant is toxic if eaten.

CLEISTOCACTUS STRAUSII AGM

syn. *Borzicactus strausii;*
Cephalocereus strausii;
Cereus strausii
Silver torch

One of the most widely available *Cleistocactus*, the silver torch produces tall, grey-green, ribbed stems covered with a coat of fine white hair-like spines. Mature plants that are over 45cm (18in) tall produce burgundy red flowers in late summer. The long, cylindrical blooms make a colourful display, emerging from sides of the stems like shooting stars.

HEIGHT & SPREAD Up to 3m x 6cm (10ft x 2½in).

CARE NOTES See opposite.

CAUTION Plant is toxic if eaten.

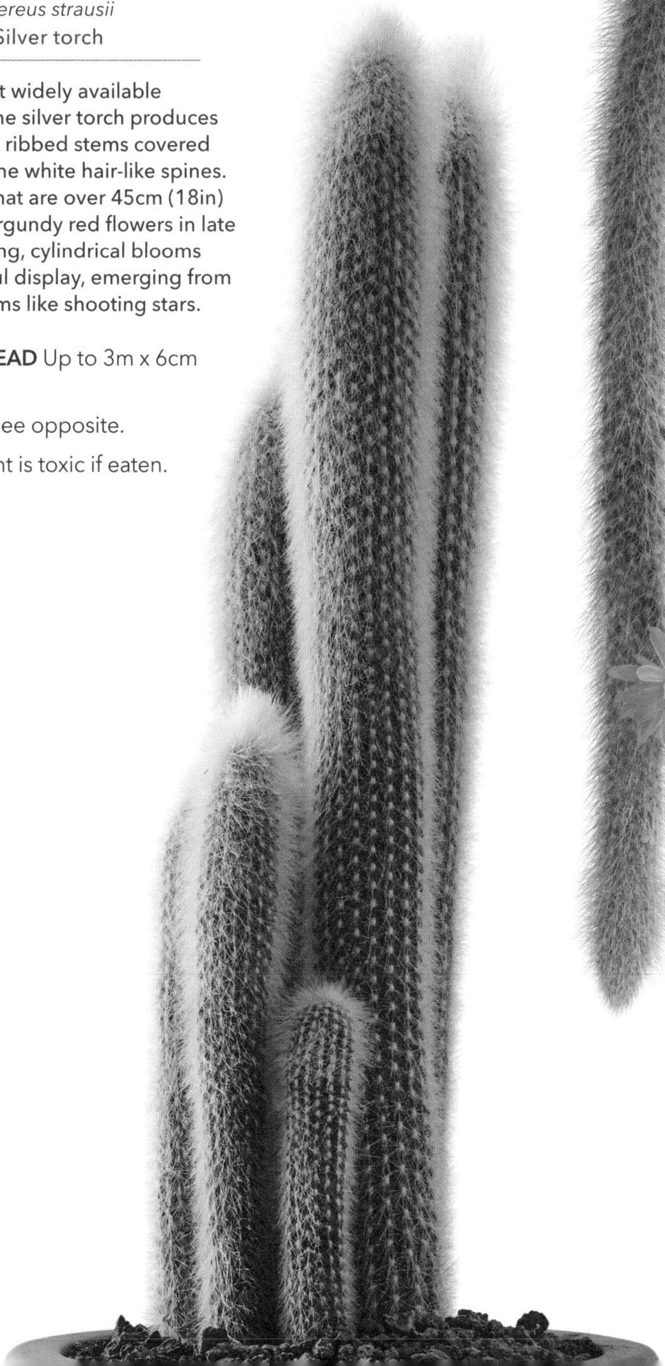

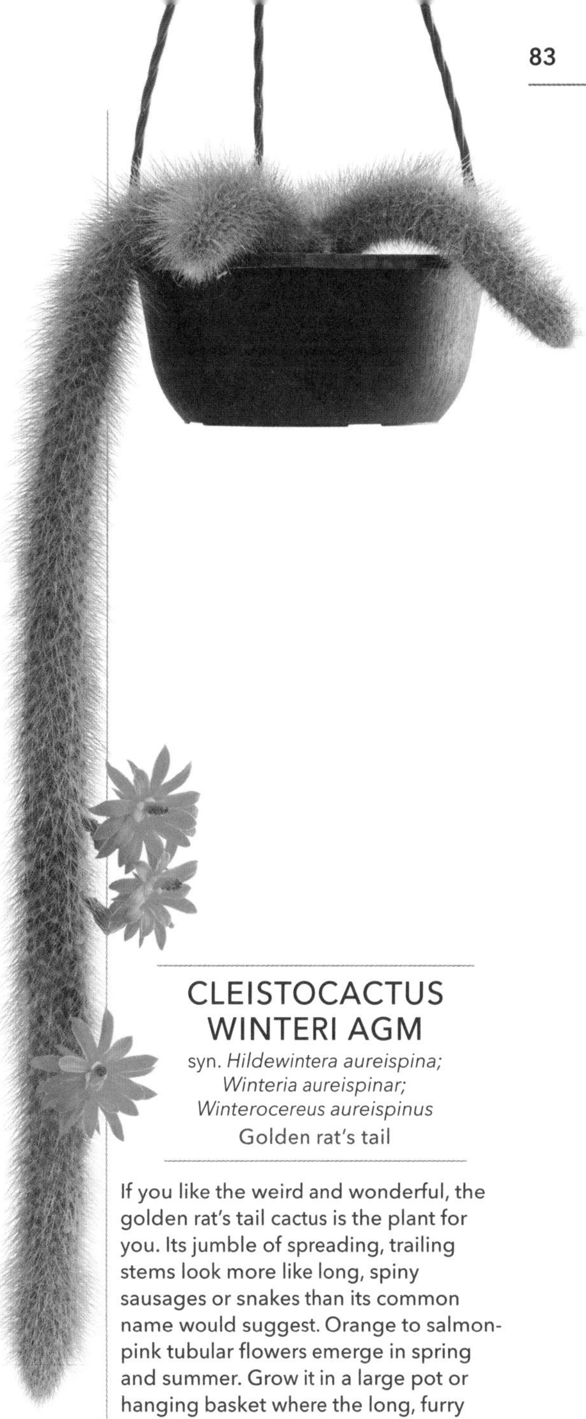

CLEISTOCACTUS WINTERI AGM

syn. *Hildewintera aureispina;*
Winteria aureispinar;
Winterocereus aureispinus
Golden rat's tail

If you like the weird and wonderful, the golden rat's tail cactus is the plant for you. Its jumble of spreading, trailing stems look more like long, spiny sausages or snakes than its common name would suggest. Orange to salmon-pink tubular flowers emerge in spring and summer. Grow it in a large pot or hanging basket where the long, furry stems can sprawl freely.

HEIGHT & SPREAD Clumps grow up to 1 x 0.6m (36in x 24in).

CARE NOTES See opposite.

CAUTION Plant is toxic if eaten.

COPIAPOA

These pretty little cacti, originally from the dry coastal deserts of northern Chile, are perfect for a small windowsill collection. The olive-brown or blue–green stems, which can be spherical or slightly columnar, typically feature well-defined ribs and black or brown spines, though a few species are spineless. As the plants mature, the stems multiply to form decorative clusters. *Copiapoa* produce tubular yellow flowers from woolly crowns at the top of the plant in summer.

TEMPERATURE 10–30°C (50–86°F)

LIGHT Position in full sun, with some shade in summer.

WATERING Water from early spring to autumn with rainwater, leaving the top 1cm (½in) of the compost to dry out between waterings. Keep the compost dry in winter.

FEEDING Apply a half-strength high-potash fertilizer once a month in spring and summer.

COMPOST Plant in cactus compost, or a 50:50 mix of loam-based (John Innes No. 2) compost and 4mm grit.

FLOWERING Plants, even young ones, will flower readily if they receive adequate water and a little fertilizer in the growing season.

PROPAGATION Sow seed or take offsets.

COMMON PROBLEMS These cacti will quickly rot in wet soil. Watch out for mealybugs and spider mite infestations.

COPIAPOA HYPOGAEA AGM

syn. *Chileorebutia hypogaea;*
Neochilenia hypogaea;
Pilocopiapoa hypogaea
Underground copiapoa

The underground copiapoa is so called because in its native Chile its round low-growing dimpled stems grow partly beneath the soil surface to protect themselves from the harsh sun. Young plants feature sparse spines that protrude from small white felted areas, giving the plant a spotty appearance. Golden-yellow scented flowers appear in summer.

HEIGHT & SPREAD Each stem grows up to 7 x 12cm (3 x 5in).

CARE NOTES See left.

CAUTION Wear cactus gloves when handling this plant.

COPIAPOA TENUISSIMA

syn. *Copiapoa humilis* subsp. *tenuissima*;
Copiapoa hypogaea subsp. *tenuissima*

The olive-green dimpled stems of this compact cactus are covered with fine hair-like spines that look like starbursts. The stems are slow to form clumps, but it flowers reliably in spring or summer when small scented yellow blooms develop at the top of the plant.

HEIGHT & SPREAD Up to 7 x 12cm (3 x 5in).

CARE NOTES See opposite.

CAUTION Wear cactus gloves when handling this plant.

CORYPHANTHA

Round or short and cylindrical, these cacti have attractive dimpled stems. While some produce just a few spines, the long, curved spines on others are the main attraction. The blooms appear in spring or summer at the top of the plant and come in shades of yellow or pink, or occasionally creamy-white. Plants remain small and compact, even when mature, making them ideal candidates where space is limited.

TEMPERATURE 5–30°C (41°F–86°F); some are frost hardy down to -10°C (14°F) if the soil is dry.

LIGHT Position in full sun, but provide some shade in midsummer.

WATERING From mid-spring to early autumn, water when the top 2cm (¾in) of compost is dry. Keep plants drier in winter, watering lightly once a month.

FEEDING Apply a half-strength high potash fertilizer fortnightly from late spring to late summer.

COMPOST Plant in cactus compost, or a 50:50 mix of loam-based (John Innes No. 2) compost and 4mm grit.

FLOWERING Mature plants will flower in summer when given sufficient fertilizer and water.

PROPAGATION Sow seed or take offsets.

COMMON PROBLEMS Prone to rotting in damp compost. Check plants regularly for mealybugs and spider mites.

CORYPHANTHA MACROMERIS

syn. *Echinocactus macromeris*;
Lepidocoryphantha macromeris;
Mammillaria macromeris

Pincushion cactus;
Big needle cactus

Hailing from the deserts of Mexico and the southern United States, the pincushion cactus is easy to grow and a great choice for a beginner. The short, cylindrical stems are dimpled and spiky, and they quickly multiply to create small clusters. Long brown needle-like spines form at the top of the plant, while shorter white spines cover the rest of the stem. The daisy-like, bright rose-pink or magenta flowers appear in the summer.

HEIGHT & SPREAD Up to 15 x 10cm (6 x 4in).

CARE NOTES See left.

CAUTION Wear cactus gloves when handling this plant.

DISOCACTUS

Dramatically different from their desert-dwelling cousins, *Disocactus* are from the tropical regions of Central America, the Caribbean, and South America, where they cling to trees and rocks. Their long trailing stems, which can be cylindrical or flat and ribbon-like, make impressive displays in hanging baskets. The large red or pink starry flowers, which appear in spring or summer, make a striking visual impression.

TEMPERATURE 6–24°C (43°F–75°F); keep at 11–14°C (52–57°F) in winter.

LIGHT Position in bright light but not direct sun, with shade from midday sun in summer.

WATERING From mid-spring to early autumn, soak the compost when watering, but reapply only when the top 1cm (½in) of compost is dry. Keep the compost just moist in winter. Mist stems occasionally to increase humidity levels.

FEEDING Use a half-strength liquid fertilizer sprayed onto the stems of the plant once every 2 weeks from early spring to autumn.

COMPOST Plant in cactus compost with added grit or perlite, or a 3:2:1 mix of loam-based compost (John Innes No. 2), 4mm grit, and peat-free multipurpose compost.

FLOWERING Move the plants to a cooler area (11–14°C/52–57°F) in winter, and keep the compost just moist, to promote flower buds to form.

PROPAGATION Sow seeds or take stem cuttings in spring.

COMMON PROBLEMS Check plants regularly for mealybugs and spider mites.

DISOCACTUS FLAGELLIFORMIS AGM

syn. *Aporocactus flagelliformis*
Rat tail cactus

One of the most widely available and easy-to-grow *Disocactus*, the trailing stems of the rat tail cactus grow quickly, soon forming a prickly fountain up to 1m (3ft) or more in length. The ribbed, cylindical stems are covered with tiny reddish-yellow spines that look like fine hairs – but beware, they are sharp and painful if touched. The spectacular crimson and pink flowers are a bonus when they appear for a few days in late spring. Display this plant in a large basket and suspend it high enough to allow the stems to develop to their full potential.

HEIGHT & SPREAD Clumps grow up to 1.5 x 0.6m (5 x 2ft).

CARE NOTES See left.

CAUTION Wear cactus gloves when handling this plant.

ECHINOCACTUS

The classic round barrel shape and neat spiny ribs makes *Echinocactus* a favourite among collectors and beginners alike. Adding colour and texture to a desert cactus display, the long yellowish, cream, or occasionally red sharp spines form along the edges of the ribs, creating distinctive prickly stripes in many species. Small flowers, which can be yellow or pink, appear like little rosettes at the top of the stems in summer.

TEMPERATURE 10–30°C (50–86°F).

LIGHT Position in full sun; provide a little shade in summer.

WATERING From mid-spring to early autumn, water only when the top 2cm (¾in) of compost is dry. Keep plants dry in winter.

FEEDING Apply a half-strength cactus fertilizer once a month during late spring and summer.

COMPOST Plant in cactus compost, or a 50:50 mix of loam-based (John Innes No. 2) compost and 4mm grit.

FLOWERING Mature plants will flower in summer, given a little fertilizer and water (see above).

PROPAGATION Sow seed.

COMMON PROBLEMS This plant is prone to root rot when grown in damp compost. Check plants regularly for aphids, mealybugs, and scale insects.

ECHINOCACTUS GRUSONII AGM
Golden barrel cactus

With its colourful prickly stems, the golden barrel cactus makes an exciting, textured feature. The pale green, heavily ribbed globes feature rows of short, densely packed yellow spines and a creamy wool top. While its classic cactus silhouette is highly appealing, the small yellow flowers are less than inspiring, often going unnoticed as they merge with the creamy-coloured "wool" at the top of the stem. This cactus generally grows a solitary stem, although older plants may form small clusters.

HEIGHT & SPREAD Up to 60 x 60cm (24 x 24in).

CARE NOTES See opposite.

CAUTION Wear cactus gloves when handling this plant.

ECHINOCEREUS

Ideal for beginners, these natives of the southern United States and Mexico are among the easiest cacti to grow. Their cylindrical stems feature spine-covered ribs; in some species, the spines are colourful or long and curved, creating an intricate lacy pattern over the entire plant. As well as the decorative stems, these pretty cacti are grown for their large, dramatic flowers, which range in colour from pinks and reds to yellows, browns, and greens; many are bicoloured too. The blooms appear in spring or summer at the top of the plant and are followed by edible fruits. Mature plants develop to form large clusters of prickly stems.

TEMPERATURE 5–30°C (41–86°F).

LIGHT Position in full sun with a little shade in midsummer.

WATERING During the spring and summer, water when the top 2cm (¾in) of compost is dry. In autumn, reduce watering to once a month, and keep plants dry in winter.

FEEDING Apply a half-strength cactus fertilizer once a month from spring to early autumn.

COMPOST Plant in cactus compost, or a 50:50 mix of loam-based (John Innes No. 2) compost and 4mm grit.

FLOWERING Keep plants on a sunny windowsill, except in the summer (see above), to encourage flowers to form.

PROPAGATION Sow seed or take offsets.

COMMON PROBLEMS Susceptible to rot if overwatered. Check regularly for mealybugs and scale insects.

ECHINOCEREUS PENTALOPHUS AGM
syn. *Cereus pentalophus*; *Cereus pentalophus* var. *radicans*; *Cereus pentalophus* var. *simplex*
Lady finger cactus; Dog tail

A must for any cactus collection, the lady finger cactus produces a mass of slim green stems that look like sprawling spiny fingers. The stems have long, sharp white or yellowish spines along the ribs, and in late spring, bright pink flowers with yellow or cream centres appear at the ends of the "fingers". The blooms are followed by edible green fruits. Grow it in a hanging basket or tall pot, where the stems and blooms can trail over the sides.

HEIGHT & SPREAD Clumps grow up to 20 x 20cm (8 x 8in).

CARE NOTES See left.

CAUTION Wear cactus gloves when handling this plant.

ECHINOCEREUS REICHENBACHII AGM

syn. *Cereus reichenbachianus;*
Echinocactus reichenbachianus;
Echinocactus reichenbachii
Black lace cactus;
Lace hedgehog cactus

Small and cylindrical, the dark green stems of the black lace cactus are often almost obscured by its multicoloured brown, black, pink, or white curved spines. These spines appear to form a lacy design, hence the plant's common name. The spines grow from ribs, which on some plants form a slightly spiralling pattern, adding to this little plant's charms. In spring or summer, large purple or pink flowers with a sweet fragrance appear at the top of each stem.

HEIGHT & SPREAD Up to 25 x 10cm (10 x 4in).

CARE NOTES See p87.

CAUTION Wear cactus gloves when handling this plant.

ECHINOCEREUS RIGIDISSIMUS subsp. RUBISPINUS

syn. *Echinocereus pectinatus*
var. *rubispinus; Echinocereus*
rigidissimus var. *rubispinus*
Rainbow cactus

The popular rainbow cactus is prized for the dark red and violet spines that cover its cylindrical stems. As if the colourful spines were not enough to catch the eye, in summer, large white-throated magenta or red flowers appear around the sides of stems. The plant also forms small clumps as it matures.

HEIGHT & SPREAD Up to 25 x 60cm (10 x 24in).

CARE NOTES See p87.

CAUTION Wear cactus gloves when handling this plant.

ECHINOCEREUS PULCHELLUS

syn. *Cereus pulchellus;*
Echinocactus pulchellus;
Echinonyctanthus pulchellus;
Echinopsis pulchella

The dainty, blue–green, globe-shaped stems of this diminutive cactus feature tiny white clusters of spines that emerge from woolly areas along the ribs, giving the plant a spotty appearance. Pink or pinkish-white daisy-like flowers appear at the top of each domed stem in summer.

HEIGHT & SPREAD Up to 6 x 7cm (2 x 2½in).

CARE NOTES See p87.

CAUTION Wear cactus gloves when handling this plant.

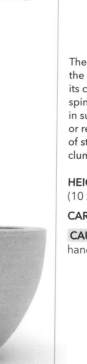

ECHINOCEREUS VIERECKII

syn. *Echinocereus viereckii subsp. viereckii*
Hedgehog cactus

The bright apple-green ribbed stems of the hedgehog cactus form dense clusters, while its yellow spines make a colourful contrast. If you have children, try the more widely available *Echinocereus viereckii* subsp. *morricalii* (pictured), which is almost spineless and safer to handle. Large, funnel-shaped magenta–purple flowers appear in summer on both species.

HEIGHT & SPREAD Each stem can reach up to 30 x 7.5cm (12 x 3in).

CARE NOTES See p87.

CAUTION Wear cactus gloves when handling this plant.

ECHINOPSIS

This group of cacti comes in a wide range of shapes and sizes, from tiny and squat to large and tree-like, but the majority are spiny, ribbed, and globe-like or cylindrical. The plants' beautiful, tubular blooms are available in many colours, including white, red, pink, violet, orange, and yellow. Although each flower only lasts a day, they appear in succession over a long period in spring and summer. The group is collectively known as hedgehog cacti, which can sometimes lead to *Echinopsis* being confused with *Echinocereus* (see pp87–88), which share the same common name.

TEMPERATURE 5–30°C (41–86°F); keep cool and dry in winter; will tolerate spells below freezing to -5°C (23°F) if the soil is dry.

LIGHT Position in full sun; provide a little shade in midsummer.

WATERING From late spring to early autumn, water when the top 2cm (¾in) of compost is dry. In autumn, reduce watering to once a month. Keep plants dry in winter.

FEEDING Apply a half-strength high-potash fertilizer every 2 weeks in summer.

COMPOST Plant in cactus compost, or a 50:50 mix of loam–based (John Innes No. 2) compost and 4mm grit.

FLOWERING Encourage plants to flower by keeping them at over 21°C (70°F) and in bright sunlight during the spring and early summer.

PROPAGATION Sow seed or take offsets.

COMMON PROBLEMS Stems will rot in damp compost. Check regularly for mealybugs and scale insects.

ECHINOPSIS CHAMAECEREUS AGM

syn. *Cereus silvestrii;*
Chamaecereus silvestrii;
Lobivia silvestrii
Peanut cactus

The peanut cactus forms clusters of short, finger-like, ribbed stems that are said to resemble the nuts after which it is named. The stems have soft spines when young but plants become spineless as they mature. Initially growing upright, they then trail slightly to make a beautiful feature in a small hanging basket. Flushes of large, dark-eyed, bright red flowers shoot out from the stems throughout spring and summer.

HEIGHT & SPREAD Up to 15 x 30cm (6 x 12in).

CARE NOTES See left.

CAUTION Wear cactus gloves when handling this plant.

ECHINOPSIS FORMOSA

syn. *Lobivia formosa;*
Soehrensia formosa

The ribbed columns of this prickly cactus are covered with long spines, which can be white, brown, or beige. The stems tend to be solitary and rarely form clusters, while the early summer flowers are normally yellow, although on some plants they may be orange or reddish-orange.

HEIGHT & SPREAD Up to 60 x 30cm (24 x 12in).

CARE NOTES See left.

CAUTION Wear cactus gloves when handling this plant.

ECHINOPSIS SUBDENUDATA 'TUFTY'

syn. *Echinopsis ancistrophora;*
Echinopsis subdenudatus
Easter lily cactus

The small, globe-shaped stems of this dainty cactus are grey–green and generally compact, although older plants are taller and more cylindrical. Safe for children to handle, this cactus is almost spineless, or has very short spines, while the marked woolly areas create its distinctive spots. The spectacular white flowers are also hard to beat, providing an almost continuous show from late spring to late summer. Sweetly fragrant, each bloom lasts just one day, but more follow in succession.

HEIGHT & SPREAD Up to 30 x 7.5cm (12 x 3in).

CARE NOTES See p89.

EPIPHYLLUM

Grown for their long, often wavy-edged, smooth-faced stems and large, orchid-like flowers, these tropical cacti have similar needs to *Disocactus* (see p86). The trailing stems form a lush, leafy display in a hanging basket, while the fragrant flowers, which appear in summer or autumn, come in a range of colours, including white, orange, red, or yellow; some are bicoloured. In Mexico this plant is prized for its edible fruits.

TEMPERATURE 6–24°C (43°F–75°F); keep at 11–14°C (52–57°F) in winter.

LIGHT Position in bright light but not direct sun. In summer, keep shaded from the midday sun.

WATERING For most of the year, soak the compost thoroughly when watering, but reapply only when the top 1cm (½in) of compost is dry. Do not water for a month during winter, to give the plant a rest period. These cacti require moderately high humidity.

FEEDING Apply cactus fertilizer every 2 weeks during spring and summer.

COMPOST Plant in cactus compost with added grit or perlite, or a 3:2:1 mix of loam-based compost (John Innes No. 2), 4mm grit, and peat-free multipurpose compost.

FLOWERING Move the plants to a cooler area (11–14°C/52–57°F) in winter, and keep the compost just moist to promote flower buds to form. Move to a warmer spot in spring.

PROPAGATION Sow seeds or take stem cuttings.

COMMON PROBLEMS Check plants regularly for mealybugs and spider mites.

EPIPHYLLUM ANGULIGER
Fishbone cactus

This deservedly popular plant produces a waterfall of unusual wavy-edged leaves that resemble fishbones, hence its common name. The white scented flowers open in the evenings in autumn — each flower lasts for just one or two days — and are followed by edible greenish fruits that taste a little like gooseberries then follow the blooms. The plant makes an attractive feature in a bright room in a hanging basket or pot on a plant stand.

HEIGHT & SPREAD Clumps grow up to 20 x 30cm (8 x 12in).

CARE NOTES See opposite.

ERIOSYCE

The spiny armour of a few *Eriosyce* species have made them very popular among collectors looking for something a little out of the ordinary. While the round globe-like or cylindrical stems are unremarkable, the plants' long, curved cream, black, or brown spines, which in some species almost cover the entire stem, draw the eye. In summer, bright pink, yellow, or cream flowers appear at the top of the plant.

TEMPERATURE 5–30°C (41–86°F); tolerates short spells below freezing to -4°C (25°F) if the soil is dry.

LIGHT Position in full sun, but provide a little light shade in midsummer.

WATERING From late spring to autumn, water when the top 2cm (¾in) of compost is dry. In autumn, reduce watering to once a month. Keep plants dry in winter.

FEEDING Apply a half-strength high-potash fertilizer every 2 weeks in summer.

COMPOST Plant in cactus compost, or a 50:50 mix of loam-based (John Innes No. 2) compost and 4mm grit.

FLOWERING Plants will flower reliably if the care advice above is followed.

PROPAGATION Sow seed.

COMMON PROBLEMS Prone to rotting if overwatered. Check regularly for mealybugs and scale insects.

ERIOSYCE SENILIS AGM
syn. *Echinocactus senilis;*
Euporteria senilis;
Neoporteria nidus f. *senilis*

Despite its diminutive size, *Eriosyce senilis* will stand out from the crowd in any cactus collection. The star attraction is the tangle of curved, bristly white spines that cover the purplish spherical or short columnar stems like candyfloss. Magenta flowers, which are not especially large, add to the plant's allure when they appear in summer.

HEIGHT & SPREAD Each stem can reach up to 18 x 8cm (7 x 3in).

CARE NOTES See left.

CAUTION Wear cactus gloves when handling this plant.

ESPOSTOA

Tall, slim, and covered with a woolly coat that protects them against the harsh climate of their native Andes, these fluffy-looking pillar-shaped plants add height and texture to a mixed cactus display. Mature plants may also produce large bell-shaped flowers in summer, followed by sweet edible fruits, although the blooms are rarely seen on *Espostoa* grown as house plants.

TEMPERATURE 12–30°C (54–86°F)

LIGHT Position in full sun, but provide light shade in midsummer.

WATERING From late spring to autumn, water when the top 1cm (½in) of compost is dry. Reduce watering in autumn. Keep compost dry in winter.

FEEDING Apply a half-strength cactus fertilizer once a month from spring to autumn.

COMPOST Plant in cactus compost, or a 50:50 mix of loam-based (John Innes No. 2) compost and 4mm grit.

FLOWERING Flowers will only appear on mature plants when exposed to sufficient sunlight.

PROPAGATION Sow seed.

COMMON PROBLEMS Prone to rotting if overwatered. Check plants regularly for mealybugs and scale insects.

ESPOSTOA LANATA AGM

syn. *Cleistocactus lanatus;
Oreocereus lanatus*
Peruvian old man cactus

The Peruvian old man cactus makes a striking silhouette, with its tall ribbed columns covered in a dense thicket of hair-like spines. Despite its cuddly appearance, this furry coat disguises sharp spines: do not be tempted to stroke it. The stems soon multiply to form clusters and mature plants will also branch out. This plant is shy to bloom, especially when grown indoors; when they do appear, the nocturnal white to purple flowers appear from late spring to early summer.

HEIGHT & SPREAD Each stem can reach up to 3m x 20cm (10ft x 8in).

CARE NOTES See left.

CAUTION Wear cactus gloves when handling this plant.

ESPOSTOA MELANOSTELE AGM

syn. *Cephalocereus melanostele;
Cereus melanostele*
Peruvian old lady cactus

Like its close cousin (see left), the Peruvian old lady cactus grows into a tall, columnar plant, with greyish-green stems covered with sharp yellow spines buried amongst fine, white, hair-like spines that look like wool. Plant in a large pot as the stems will soon multiply to fill it. The white flowers rarely appear on cacti grown as house plants.

HEIGHT & SPREAD Clusters grow up to 1 x 0.6m (3 x 2ft).

CARE NOTES See left.

CAUTION Wear cactus gloves when handling this plant.

FEROCACTUS

Natives of the southern United States and Mexico, this group of cacti are popular for their chubby barrel shape, and fierce, spiny armour. The ribbed stems are adorned with thick, sharp spines that may be hooked or straight, and in a few species, bright pink or red. The small, funnel-shaped flowers come in yellow, purple, or red, with buds emerging through the dense spiny thickets in summer. Keep this group of cacti out of reach of children and pets.

TEMPERATURE 10–30°C (64–86°F); keep plants cool at 10–12°C (54–50°F) from late autumn to late winter.

LIGHT Position in full sun, with a little shade in midsummer.

WATERING From spring to early autumn, allow the top 2cm (¾in) of the compost to dry out before watering, then water well and leave to drain. From late autumn to late winter, keep compost almost dry.

FEEDING Apply a diluted cactus fertilizer every 3–4 weeks from spring to early autumn.

COMPOST Plant in a cactus compost or mixture of a 3:1:1 mix of soil-based compost, sand, and perlite.

FLOWERING Plants will flower given sufficient light and a little fertilizer.

PROPAGATION Sow seed.

COMMON PROBLEMS Susceptible to rotting in wet compost or a humid atmosphere. Mealybugs and scale insects may be a problem.

FEROCACTUS EMORYI subsp. RECTISPINUS

syn. *Ferocactus rectispinus*; *Echinocactus emoryi* var. *rectispinus*; *Echinocactus rectispinus*
Long-spined barrel cactus

With its armour of terrifying red spines measuring up to 25cm (10in) in length, the long-spined barrel cactus is aptly named. While the spines are a guaranteed talking point, the plant also produces beautiful large pale yellow flowers in summer. Take care to avoid injury when displaying this cactus – a shelf wider than the spines out of reach of children and pets would be best.

HEIGHT & SPREAD Up to 60 x 30cm (24 x 12in).

CARE NOTES See left.

CAUTION Wear cactus gloves when handling this plant.

FEROCACTUS FORDII subsp. BOREALIS AGM

syn. *Echinocactus fordii*
Ford barrel cactus

Impossible to overlook when in bloom, the colourful Ford barrel cactus creates a focal point in a collection, or you could display it as a feature plant on its own. Its long, dramatic, red-tinged curved spines, surrounded by thinner white spines, grow in starry clusters along grey-green ribs, while large purplish-pink flowers appear at the top of the plant in summer. For a similar cactus with even longer, sword-like spines, look out for the true species, *Ferocactus fordii*.

HEIGHT & SPREAD Up to 45 x 30cm (18 x 12in).

CARE NOTE See left.

CAUTION Wear cactus gloves when handling this plant.

FEROCACTUS GLAUCESCENS AGM

syn. *Ferocactus pfeifferi;*
Echinocactus glaucescens;
Echinocactus pfeifferi
Glaucous barrel cactus

The bluish colour and rounded shape of young plants give the glaucous barrel cactus its common name, although it may develop a more cylindrical silhouette as it matures. Easy to grow, this cactus has long yellow spines that sprout from the edges of well-defined ribs in starry clusters, while long-lasting funnel-shaped yellow flowers appear in summer. The stems of this decorative cactus soon multiply to form clusters.

HEIGHT & SPREAD Up to 60 x 50cm (24 x 20in).

CARE NOTES See p93.

CAUTION Wear cactus gloves when handling this plant.

FEROCACTUS GRACILIS AGM

syn. *Ferocactus peninsulae* var. *gracilis*
Fire barrel cactus

With its dramatic bright pink spines, the colourful fire barrel cactus is one to look out for. Like its cousins, young plants are spherical, becoming more columnar as they mature, but the stems are very slow to produce clusters. Pinky-red flowers appear in early summer at the top of the plant.

HEIGHT & SPREAD Up to 60 x 30cm (24 x 12in).

CARE NOTES See p93. Bring plants into more light in summer if the spines start to lose their colouration.

CAUTION Wear cactus gloves when handling this plant.

FEROCACTUS LATISPINUS AGM

syn. *Ferocactus latispinus* var. *latispinus;*
Echinocactus cornigerus var. *latispinus;*
Echinocactus latispinus
Devil's tongue cactus

It's easy to see how the devil's tongue cactus came by its common name: one of its curved red spines is larger and longer than the others, like a tongue sticking out. When combined with smaller red and creamy-white spines, this produces a stunning effect. The blue-green ribbed stem of this barrel cactus also maintains a more rounded shape than many other mature ferocactus. Purplish-pink flowers develop in summer on established plants.

HEIGHT & SPREAD Up to 25 x 25cm (10 x 10in).

CARE NOTES See p93.

CAUTION Wear cactus gloves when handling this plant.

FEROCACTUS MACRODISCUS

syn. *Echinocactus macrodiscus*
Candy cactus

As the candy cactus matures, it produces a low, wide, domed stem that sets it apart from the more rounded plants in this group. The grey-green ribs also sport curved, cream-coloured spines. While these are not as spectacular as the spines of some barrel cacti, the large white and pink striped flowers help to compensate when they appear in spring, even on young plants.

HEIGHT & SPREAD Up to 10 x 25cm (4 x 10in).

CARE NOTES See p93.

CAUTION Wear cactus gloves when handling this plant.

FEROCACTUS VIRIDESCENS AGM

syn. *Echinocactus viridescens*
Coast barrel cactus

The coast barrel cactus has a pleasing rounded shape and bright green ribbed stems. Its curved yellow spines are pink when young, giving the plant a two-tone look, and in early summer, green or red-tinged flowers appear. Use this unassuming cactus as a foil for more brightly coloured types.

HEIGHT & SPREAD Up to 25 x 30cm (10 x 12in).

CARE NOTES See p93.

CAUTION Wear cactus gloves when handling this plant.

GYMNOCALYCIUM

Perfect for a narrow windowsill, these easy-care South American cacti are round and compact, with white, brown or black spines that radiate from woolly areas on the ribs. The stems are grey–green or blue–green, and in some species the ribs are unusually wide, dividing the plant into triangular segments that look like little chins, hence the common name, "chin cactus". Most *Gymnocalycium* plants produce white, cream, or pale pink flowers in spring or summer, although some of the most popular species have dark red or yellow blooms.

TEMPERATURE 10–30°C (50–86°F); some species tolerate temperatures down to -15°C (5°F).

LIGHT Position in full sun, and in light shade in summer.

WATERING From late spring to early autumn, allow the top 1cm (½in) of the compost to dry out before watering, then water well and leave to drain. Do not water from late autumn to late winter.

FEEDING Apply a half-strength high-potash fertilizer once a month from spring to late summer.

COMPOST Plant in a cactus compost or mixture of a 3:1:1 mix of soil-based compost, sand, and perlite.

FLOWERING Plants will flower readily but need high heat and good light to open; increase exposure to sunlight if flowers fail to form.

PROPAGATION Sow seed.

COMMON PROBLEMS Prone to rotting in damp compost. Check plants regularly for mealybugs.

GYMNOCALYCIUM BALDIANUM AGM

syn. *Echinocactus baldianus; Gymnocalycium platense* var. *baldianum; Gymnocalycium venturianum*
Dwarf chin cactus; Spider cactus

Free-flowering and easy to grow, the dwarf chin cactus is ideal for beginners. Unlike those of many of its cousins, the ribs of this *Gymnocalycium* have a more dimpled surface, from which sprout pale brown spines that look like tiny spiders, giving rise to its other common name. The large purple–red or pinkish-purple early summer flowers are produced when plants are quite young.

HEIGHT & SPREAD Up to 10 x 13cm (4 x 5in).

CARE NOTES See left.

CAUTION Wear cactus gloves when handling this plant.

GYMNOCALYCIUM BALDIANUM var. ALBIFLORUM

syn. *Gymnocalycium kieslingii*
White-flowered dwarf chin cactus

Almost identical to *Gymnocalycium baldianum* (see right), and equally easy to grow, this variety produces elegant white flowers in summer that create a striking contrast to the dark blue-green stems.

HEIGHT & SPREAD Up to 10 x 13cm (4 x 5in).

CARE NOTES See left.

CAUTION Wear cactus gloves when handling this plant.

GYMNOCALYCIUM BRUCHII AGM

syn. *Astrophytum bruchii;*
Frailea bruchi
Chin cactus

This miniature cactus has round flat-topped blue-green stems, and the ribs are covered with long, curved white spines. The flowers, which appear in clusters in spring at the top of the plant like a bouquet of tiny water lilies, are an unusual shade of lavender-white. Inedible green fruits follow the blooms. This cactus is hardier than most, tolerating -15°C (5°F) if the soil is dry.

HEIGHT & SPREAD Up to 4 x 6cm (1½ x 2½in).

CARE NOTES See opposite.

CAUTION Wear cactus gloves when handling this plant.

GYMNOCALYCIUM CALOCHLORUM

syn. *Echinocactus calochlorus;*
Gymnocalycium proliferum var.
calochlorum; Gymnocalycium
quehlianum var. *calochlorum*
Clustering chin cactus

Highly prized for its small, round, dimpled stems, the clustering chin cactus is covered in white curved spines that produce a pretty lacy pattern over the surface. The large, elegant pale pink to white flowers, which appear on spineless tubes in late spring or summer, are followed by inedible green fruits. It forms small clusters of stems after a few years.

HEIGHT & SPREAD Up to 4 x 6cm (1½ x 2½in).

CARE NOTES See opposite.

CAUTION Wear cactus gloves when handling this plant.

GYMNOCALYCIUM HORSTII var. BUENEKERI

syn. *Gymnocalycium buenekeri*
Chin cactus

This chin cactus has the classic wide-ribbed rounded shape that gives *Gymnocalycium* their common name. Sparse long yellow curved spines contrast with the blue-green stems, which multiply quickly to produce small clumps. Large pale pink flowers appear in summer. This cactus is frost-resistant down to -4°C (25°F) if the soil is dry.

HEIGHT & SPREAD Up to 10 x 10cm (4 x 4in).

CARE NOTES See opposite.

CAUTION Wear cactus gloves when handling this plant.

HATIORA

These tropical cacti are epiphytes, which means they grow on the surface of another plant. In their native Brazil, their spineless stems use the tree trunks as props to keep them off the forest floor where they would be vulnerable to damage. In some species, the stems are cylindrical, but on the most popular types they are flattened and divided into segments. Large showy flowers appear in spring.

TEMPERATURE 7–24°C (45–75°F); in winter, keep plants cool at 7–18°C (45–65°F).

LIGHT Position in bright , indirect sun. Provide in light shade in summer.

WATERING From early spring to early autumn, soak the compost thoroughly when watering, but only reapply when the top 1cm (½in) of compost is dry. Keep the compost just moist in winter. These cacti need moderately high humidity.

FEEDING Apply a half-strength balanced fertilizer fortnightly during spring and summer.

COMPOST Plant in cactus compost with added grit or perlite, or a 3:2:1 mix of loam-based compost (John Innes No. 2), 4mm grit, and peat-free multipurpose compost.

FLOWERING Move the plants to a cooler area in winter: 10–18°C (50–65°F) during the day and 7–13°C (45–55°F) at night, and keep the compost just moist to encourage flower buds to form. Return them to a warmer area in spring.

PROPAGATION Sow seeds or take stem cuttings.

COMMON PROBLEMS Check plants for mealybugs and spider mites.

HATIORA GAERTNERI AGM

syn. *Epiphyllum gaertneri;*
Epiphyllum russellianum var. *gaertneri;*
Rhipsalidopsis gaertneri;
Schlumbergera gaertneri
Easter cactus

One of the most popular *Hatiora*, the Easter cactus is so called because of its flowering time, which generally coincides with this Christian festival in spring. It produces green flattened trailing stems, made up of segments with small notches along the edges. Grow it in a hanging basket where you can appreciate the starry scarlet, orange, or pink flowers (depending on the cultivar), which last for several weeks.

HEIGHT & SPREAD Up to 50 x 30 cm (20 x 12in).

CARE NOTES See left.

LEUCHTENBERGIA

This cactus group includes just one species, *Leuchtenbergia principis*, which is native to the Chihuahaun desert in Mexico. An excellent choice for those searching for an unusual addition to their collection, the three-sided stems resemble the leaves of an agave, giving rise to its common name of "agave cactus". Pale yellow flowers appear on mature plants in the summer months.

TEMPERATURE -8–30°C (18–86°F).

LIGHT Position in full sun.

WATERING From autumn to late spring, apply plenty of water when the top 1cm (½in) of compost is dry. Do not water in winter.

FEEDING Apply a half-strength cactus fertilizer once a month during spring and summer.

COMPOST Plant in cactus compost.

FLOWERING Plants are more likely to flower if grown outside in summer, where they can benefit from stronger direct sunlight.

PROPAGATION Sow seed.

COMMON PROBLEMS Damp compost will cause stems to rot. Check regularly for scale insects, mealybugs, and spider mites.

LEUCHTENBERGIA PRINCIPIS
Agave cactus

Not everyone's idea of a beautiful plant, the agave cactus is notable for its strange appearance. Soft, papery spines grow in tufts from the ends of the stem sections, while large fragrant pale yellow flowers appear in summer. Each bloom lasts only two or three days, but they appear in succession over many weeks.

HEIGHT & SPREAD Up to 60 x 30cm (24 x 12in).

CARE NOTES See opposite.

LOPHOPHORA

Small and elegant, but these low-growing, globe-shaped cacti look like tiny apples. There are just two species in this group: *Lophophora diffusa*, which has smooth yellow-green stems, and *Lophophora williamsii*, with dimpled blue-green ribbed stems. Both are spineless but feature soft creamy-coloured wool that in some plants looks like tufts of hair sprouting in patches over the stems. Slow to flower, mature lophophora plants produce small pale pink blooms in summer from a woolly area at the top of the plant.

TEMPERATURE 5–40°C (41–104°F); will tolerate freezing temperatures of -7°C (20°F) if the soil is dry.

LIGHT Position in full sun and provide light shade in summer.

WATERING Water well during the summer months, but allow the top 1cm (½in) of compost to dry out between waterings; water sparingly in spring and autumn and do not water at all in winter.

FEEDING Apply a half-strength cactus fertilizer twice in summer.

COMPOST Plant in cactus compost with added grit or perlite, or a 3:2:1 mix of loam-based compost (John Innes No. 2), 4mm grit, and peat-free multipurpose compost.

FLOWERING Flowers appear on plants that are at least 5 years old. Keep in a warm room in direct sunlight, and leave unwatered for several weeks in early spring, then water well.

PROPAGATION Sow seed.

COMMON PROBLEMS Prone to rotting if overwatered. Check plants regularly for mealybugs.

LOPHOPHORA WILLIAMSII
syn. *Echinocactus lewinii;*
Echinocactus williamsii;
Echinocactus williamsii var. *anhaloninicus;*
Echinocactus williamsii var. *pellotinicus*
Dumpling cactus; Peyote

The hair-like wool that dots the surface of the dumpling cactus can be long and tufty in some plants, while in others, it is barely noticeable. The stems slowly multiply to make attractive clusters, and when mature, plants produce pale pink flowers in summer. Plant in a deep pot to accommodate the large root.

HEIGHT & SPREAD Up to 6 x 12cm (2½ x 4½in).

CARE NOTES See left.

CAUTION Plant is toxic if eaten.

MAMMILLARIA

One of the most popular and widely available groups of cacti, *Mammillaria* includes over 200 species and varieties. Most are globe- or ball-shaped, although a few form short cylindrical columns, and they either grow as solitary stems or in domed clusters. The spines may be stiff and stout, or hair-like, and some plants also feature wool or bristles. The flowers tend to be small and appear in rings around the stems, producing a beautiful haloed effect. They also come in a wide range of colours.

TEMPERATURE 5–30°C (41–86°F).

LIGHT Position in full sun, but provide some shade in summer.

WATERING From spring to autumn, water thoroughly but allow the top 1–2cm (½–¾in) of compost to dry out between waterings. Do not water in winter, but mist plants occasionally.

FEEDING Apply a half-strength cactus fertilizer once a month from spring to early autumn.

COMPOST Plant in cactus compost with added grit or perlite, or a 3:2:1 mix of loam-based compost (John Innes No. 2), 4mm grit, and peat-free multipurpose compost.

FLOWERING To encourage flowering, keep plants in a cool place in winter and do not water. Then, in spring, resume watering and increase the temperature.

PROPAGATION Sow seed or take offsets.

COMMON PROBLEMS Plants are susceptible to rotting if overwatered. Check plants regularly for mealybugs.

MAMMILLARIA BAUMII AGM

syn. *Dolichothele baumii;*
Ebnerella baumii
Pincushion cactus

Starry clusters of soft white spines cover this little rounded cactus like spun sugar, almost obscuring the grey-green stems. It soon forms small clumps, which are decorated with relatively large, scented golden-yellow flowers in late spring.

HEIGHT & SPREAD Each stem grows up to 7 x 15cm (3½ x 6in).

CARE NOTES See left.

CAUTION Wear cactus gloves when handling this plant.

MAMMILLARIA BOMBYCINA AGM

syn. *Chilita bombycina; Ebnerella bombycine; Escobariopsis bombycine; Neomammillaria bombycina*
Silken pincushion cactus

The short cylindrical stems of the silken pincushion cactus quickly multiply to form large dome-shaped clusters. Each stem is covered in a mass of short white spines and longer brown curved spines that protrude from a downy base to create a fascinating spotty, two-tone effect. Circular clusters of magenta-pink flowers appear on the upper surfaces of the stems in spring and summer.

HEIGHT & SPREAD Clumps grow up to 20 x 30cm (8 x 12in).

CARE NOTES See left.

CAUTION Wear cactus gloves when handling this plant.

MAMMILLARIA ELONGATA AGM

syn. *Leptocladia elongate;*
Leptocladodia elongata;
Neomammillaria elongata
Ladyfinger cactus;
Golden star cactus

MAMMILLARIA CARMENAE AGM

syn. *Escobariopsis carmenae*
Isla Carmen pincushion cactus

The Isla Carmen pincushion cactus produces small dimpled globes covered with dense clusters of soft fine white or pale yellow spines that look like sparkling starbursts. In spring and summer, small yellow-centred white or pink-tinged flowers appear in a halo around the top of the plant.

HEIGHT & SPREAD Each stem grows up to 10 x 10cm (4 x 4in).

CARE NOTES See opposite.

CAUTION Wear cactus gloves when handling this plant.

The popular ladyfinger cactus produces clusters of prickly finger-like stems adorned with a network of creamy-yellow to brown curved spines. The upright or slightly trailing stems make this little cactus a good candidate for a hanging basket. Small pale yellow or pink-tinged blooms appear in spring.

HEIGHT & SPREAD Clusters grow up to 15 x 20cm (6 x 8in).

CARE NOTES See opposite.

CAUTION Wear cactus gloves when handling this plant.

MAMMILLARIA HAHNIANA AGM

syn. *Neomammillaria hahniana*
Old lady of Mexico

The long, soft, silvery spines that cloak the old lady of Mexico look like wispy hair. Globe-shaped or short and cylindrical, this cactus flowers prolifically, even when young, producing an abundance of rose-red blooms in spring, followed by inedible red fruits. Easy to grow, this is an ideal choice for beginners.

HEIGHT & SPREAD Clusters grow up to 10 x 20cm (4 x 8in).

CARE NOTES See opposite.

CAUTION Wear cactus gloves when handling this plant.

MAMMILLARIA LONGIFLORA

syn. *Neomammillaria longiflora;*
Phellosperma longiflora
Pincushion cactus

Squat, round, and dimpled when young, the stems of this cactus become slightly taller and more domed-shaped with age. Short white spines, with a longer reddish-brown hooked spine in the centre of each cluster, give it a colourful spidery look. The pink funnel- or bell-shaped flowers are often as big as the stem.

HEIGHT & SPREAD Up to 6 x 9cm (2½ x 3½in).

CARE NOTES See p100.

CAUTION Wear cactus gloves when handling this plant.

MAMMILLARIA MAGNIMAMMA AGM

syn. *Mammillaria centricirrha*
var. *magnimamma;*
Neomammillaria magnimamma
Mexican pincushion

The curved spines of the Mexican pincushion can vary from plant to plant, with some as long as 5cm (2in), while others are much shorter. The spines cover globe-shaped, grey-green stems, which soon multiply to form mounded clusters. White or cream flowers, which have delicate red or purplish-pink veining, develop in rings at the top of the stems in spring.

HEIGHT & SPREAD Clusters grow up to 30 x 45cm (12 x 18in).

CARE NOTES See p100.

CAUTION Wear cactus gloves when handling this plant.

MAMMILLARIA PLUMOSA AGM

syn. *Escobariopsis plumosa;*
Neomammillaria plumosa
Feather cactus

At first glance, the feather cactus does not really look like a plant at all, as it is covered with dense clusters of fine, downy-looking spines that completely disguise the small round stems. In fact, this feathery cloak evolved to protect the plant from the blistering sun of its native Mexico. Small creamy-white or pale pink flowers, which are sweetly scented, appear at the top of the stems in late summer.

HEIGHT & SPREAD Clusters grow up to 10 x 40cm (4 x 16in).

CARE NOTES See p100.

CAUTION Wear cactus gloves when handling this plant.

MAMMILLARIA SPINOSISSIMA AGM

syn. *Mammillaria spinosissima* f. *rubrispina;*
Neomammillaria spinosissima
Spiny pincushion cactus

Rusty red bristly spines are produced at the top of the spiny pincushion cactus, while shorter and finer white spines cover the rest of the plant. The stems are round or form short columns, and they quickly multiply to create decorative clusters. Haloes of small purplish or pink flowers appear at the top of the stems in spring.

HEIGHT & SPREAD Clusters grow up to 10 x 30cm (4 x 12in).

CARE NOTES See p100.

CAUTION Wear gloves when handling this plant.

MAMMILLARIA ZEILMANNIANA AGM

syn. *Mammillaria crinita* f. *zeilmanniana;*
Neomammillaria zeilmanniana
Rose pincushion

The rose pincushion cactus quickly forms eye-catching clusters of prickly pink-hued globes. The effect is produced by long reddish spines, surrounded by fine white spines, which cover the round to short cylindrical green stems. Each stem is topped with a ring of rosy-purple flowers in summer, although the blooms can appear at other times of the year too.

HEIGHT & SPREAD Up to 12 x 20cm (5 x 8in).

CARE NOTES See p100.

CAUTION Wear cactus gloves when handling this plant.

MATUCANA

A good choice for beginners, *Matucana* are globe-shaped or short cylindrical plants with bright green or blue–green stems. Some species are spineless when mature; others produce clusters of long, sharp spines, that can be yellow, white, black, or brown. Plants flower at an early age, the funnel-shaped blooms (some larger than the stems) appearing at the top of the plant in late spring or summer. The flowers come in a range of colours, but are most commonly red, yellow, or pink.

TEMPERATURE 10–30°C (50–86°F).

LIGHT Position in full sun; provide a light shade in midsummer.

WATERING During the spring and summer, water when the top 2cm (¾in) of compost is dry. In autumn, reduce watering to once a month. Keep plants dry in winter.

FEEDING Apply a half-strength cactus fertilizer once in spring.

COMPOST Plant in cactus compost, or a 50:50 mix of loam-based (John Innes No. 2) compost and 4mm grit. Plant in a relatively deep pot to accommodate the roots.

FLOWERING Stand plants in full sun and provide good air circulation to encourage them to bloom.

PROPAGATION Sow seed or take offsets.

COMMON PROBLEMS These plants will rot in wet compost. Check plants regularly for mealybugs and spider mites.

MATUCANA AURANTIACA AGM

syn. *Arequipa aurantiaca;*
Borzicactus aurantiacus;
Echinocactus aurantiacus;
Submatucana aurantiaca
Orange matucana

The orange matucana forms a cluster of small, globe-shaped, light green stems with long, reddish-brown spines radiating out from woolly areas along the ribs. The large orange-red flowers can reach up to 10cm (4in) in length, dwarfing the little stems and producing a dazzling display when they appear in summer.

HEIGHT & SPREAD Each stem grows up to 15 x 15cm (6 x 6in).

CARE NOTES See left.

CAUTION Wear cactus gloves when handling this plant.

MATUCANA AUREIFLORA

syn. *Borzicactus aureiflorus;*
Submatucana aureiflora

The unusual spines and bright flowers make this prickly flat-topped globe popular with cactus enthusiasts. Clusters of long, curved spines decorate the ribs and are amber coloured at the base and almost translucent at the tips. Several flushes of large, golden–yellow flowers appear in spring and summer, and unusually for cacti, they remain open day and night.

HEIGHT & SPREAD Each stem grows up to 10 x 12cm (4 x 5in).

CARE NOTES See left.

CAUTION Wear cactus gloves when handling this plant.

MATUCANA INTERTEXTA AGM
syn. *Borzicactus intertextus;*
Submatucana intertexta

Resembling a round green coral covered with baby sea urchins, this pretty little cactus is shaped like a spiky ball. Clusters of curved, brown-tipped, white spines create the sea-urchin effect, while tubular orange flowers appear in late spring or early summer.

HEIGHT & SPREAD Each stem grows up to 20 x 18cm (8 x 7in).

CARE NOTES See opposite.

CAUTION Wear cactus gloves when handling this plant.

MATUCANA KRAHNII
syn. *Borzicactus krahnii*

The grey-green, globe-shaped stems of this diminutive cactus soon form small clusters, but the plant will remain compact and suitable for a narrow windowsill even when mature. The knobbly ribs feature black- and brown-tipped spines, and bouquets of small, bright red flowers appear in flushes over a few weeks in spring and summer.

HEIGHT & SPREAD Each stem grows up to 8 x 8cm (3 x 3in).

CARE NOTES See opposite.

CAUTION Wear cactus gloves when handling this plant.

MATUCANA POLZII
syn. *Matucana aurantiaca* subsp. *polziiare*

Quick to form offsets, the baby plants of this small cactus nestle around the mother stem, giving it a quirky look. The dark red to orange funnel-shaped blooms it produces are quite showy, but only appear on mature stems.

HEIGHT & SPREAD Clusters grow up to 5 x 15 cm (2 x 6in).

CARE NOTES See opposite.

MELOCACTUS

Despite its resemblance to desert cacti, *Melocactus* are tropical plants, hailing from the Caribbean and Central and South America. Not the easiest to grow, those willing to nurture them will be rewarded with beautiful spiny stems topped with unusual red or white bristly areas (known as "cephalium") that are said to resemble little fez hats. When the cephalium appears, the stem stops growing but the caps continue to develop. Small flowers grow from the cephalium, followed by large edible red or pink tubular fruits that look like candles.

TEMPERATURE 12–30°C (54–86°F).

LIGHT Position in full sun, with some shade in summer.

WATERING Keep the compost moist from late spring to late summer, reapplying water when the top of the compost feels dry. Keep plants slightly moist in autumn and winter; do not allow the compost to dry out completely.

FEEDING Apply a half-strength balanced liquid fertilizer every 2 weeks from spring to autumn.

COMPOST Plant in cactus compost with added perlite.

FLOWERING Flowers appear on mature plants grown in good light in a well-ventilated area in moist, but not wet compost.

PROPAGATION Sow seed.

COMMON PROBLEMS These plants will rot in wet compost. Pests to look out for include mealybugs and spider mites.

MELOCACTUS MATANZANUS
Turk's cap cactus

One of the smallest and most popular *Melocactus*, the Turk's cap cactus flowers when quite young form red cephalium (see left) at the top of the plant. Starry clusters of brown or white spines form in vertical lines on ribbed globe-shaped stems. A ring of small rose-pink flowers, followed by lilac-pink fruits emerge on 4- to 5-year-old plants. Buy one in flower if you want to be sure of blooms.

HEIGHT & SPREAD Each stem grows up to 18 x 9cm (7 x 3½in).

CARE NOTES See left.

CAUTION Wear cactus gloves when handling this plant.

OPUNTIA

One of the most recognizable of all cactus groups, *Opuntia* range from compact, low-growing, spreading plants to tree-sized species that reach 5m (16ft) or more in the wild. The stems are made up of distinctive flat, paddle-shaped segments, known as "cladodes", which are protected by clusters of fine, hair-like prickles (glochids) that irritate the skin when touched. Some species also produce longer spines. Known as prickly pears due to their red edible fruits, these cacti also produce beautiful yellow, pink, or orange flowers in spring or summer.

TEMPERATURE 5–30°C (41–86°F); some species are frost-hardy down to -10°C (14°F) if the soil is dry.

LIGHT Position in full sun all year.

WATERING During the spring and summer, water when the top 2cm (¾in) of compost is dry. Reduce watering in autumn. Keep plants dry in winter.

FEEDING Apply a half-strength cactus fertilizer once a month from spring to autumn.

COMPOST Plant in cactus compost, or a 50:50 mix of loam-based (John Innes No. 2) compost and 4mm grit.

FLOWERING Flowers can appear on mature plants, but need high light levels and lower winter temperatures to develop.

PROPAGATION Sow seed or take cuttings.

COMMON PROBLEMS These plants will rot in wet compost. Pests to look out for include mealybugs and spider mites.

OPUNTIA CANTABRIGIENSIS

syn. *Opuntia engelmannii* var. *cuija*
Engelman prickly pear

If you buy two Engelman prickly pear plants, you may find that they look slightly different, as there is some variation in this species, but all form spreading shrub-like plants comprised of oval or round stem segments. This is a large cactus and needs space to show off its elegant shape and long, sharp spines. Large yellow flowers appear in spring and are followed by reddish-purple, pear-shaped fruits.

HEIGHT & SPREAD Up to 0.9 x 1.2m (3 x 4ft).

CARE NOTES See opposite; keep at or just above 10–18°C (50–65°F) in winter.

CAUTION Wear cactus gloves when handling this plant.

OPUNTIA MICRODASYS 'ALBATA' AGM

syn. *Opuntia microdasys* var. *albispina*
White bunny ear's cactus

A beautiful cultivar of the species *Opuntia microdasys* (see left), 'Albata' has white polka-dot glochids, which look like snow sprinkled over the stems. Lemon-yellow flowers appear in summer, followed by red fruits. They may appear beautiful and inviting but do not touch them, as the glochids are painful and difficult to remove from the skin.

HEIGHT & SPREAD Up to 45 x 60cm (18 x 24in).

CARE NOTES See opposite.

CAUTION Wear cactus gloves when handling this plant.

OPUNTIA MICRODASYS AGM

Bunny ears cactus;
Polka dot cactus

Its relatively small size and cartoon-like silhouette makes the bunny ears cactus a favourite among collectors and beginners alike. Evenly spaced spots of glochids form a polka-dot pattern – hence its other common name – while the oval stem segments always appear in pairs like rabbit's ears. Do not be tempted to touch the plant. It may look soft and cute but, as with all *Opuntia*, the prickles irritate the skin. Yellow flowers form along the edges of the pads in summer and are followed by purple to red fruits.

HEIGHT & SPREAD Up to 45 x 60cm (18 x 24in).

CARE NOTES See opposite.

CAUTION Wear cactus gloves when handling this plant.

OPUNTIA MONACANTHA

syn. *Cactus monacanthos*
Drooping prickly pear

In the wild, the drooping prickly pear is a tree-like cactus. Growing it in a pot will restrict its size, but make sure you can display it where the large spiky branched stems will not cause injury. The plant forms a short trunk and slim, oval- to oblong-shaped green stem segments, covered with long, sharp brown spines that detach easily when touched. The yellow or orange flowers appear in late spring and are followed by pear-shaped, reddish-purple fruits.

HEIGHT & SPREAD Up to 90 x 80cm (3 x 2½ft).

CARE NOTES See p107.

CAUTION Wear cactus gloves when handling this plant.

OREOCEREUS

The name *Oreocereus* means "mountain cereus", and refers to its natural home high up in Andes Mountains in South America. To protect it from this harsh environment, the short columnar stems are covered with a white woolly coat that looks like fine hair, with long, sharp spines hidden among the soft wrapping. In spring, this cactus produces dazzling red or orange flowers.

TEMPERATURE 5–30°C (41–86°F); plants will tolerate -10°C (14°F) if the soil is dry.

LIGHT Position in full sun, but provide some shade in summer.

WATERING During the spring and summer, water when the top 2cm (¾in) of compost is dry. In autumn, reduce watering. Keep plants dry in winter.

FEEDING Apply a half-strength cactus fertilizer once a month from spring to late summer.

COMPOST Plant in cactus compost, or a 50:50 mix of loam-based (John Innes No. 2) compost and 4mm grit.

FLOWERING Flowers only appear on mature plants; buy one in flower to guarantee blooms.

PROPAGATION Sow seed.

COMMON PROBLEMS These plants will rot in wet compost. Check them regularly for pests, particularly mealybugs and spider mites.

OREOCEREUS CELSIANUS
syn. *Borzicactus celsianus;*
Cereus celsianus;
Cleistocactus celsianus;
Pilocereus celsianus
Old man of the Andes

The ribbed columnar stems of the old man of the Andes are covered with silky white hairs that are more profuse towards the top of the plant. Yellowish-brown spines protrude from the fuzzy coat like sharp needles. In spring, funnel-shaped blooms, which are pale purplish-pink to dark red, appear along the stem.

HEIGHT & SPREAD Up to 60 x 8cm (24 x 3in).

CARE NOTES See opposite.

CAUTION Wear cactus gloves when handling this plant.

OROYA

Hailing from the Andes, these cacti are named after the Peruvian town of la Oroya where they were first discovered. The beautiful spiky globes or short, fat columns, which can grow up to 30cm (12in) in diameter, make dramatic displays on a wide windowsill or under a skylight. The ribs are covered with long curved spines, while a ring of small yellow or pink flowers, held on long pink or red stems, appears at the top of the plant in spring or summer.

TEMPERATURE 5–30°C (41–86°F); some species will tolerate -7°C (19°F) if the soil is dry.

LIGHT Position in full sun for most of the year, but provide some shade in summer.

WATERING During the spring and summer, water when the top 2cm (¾in) of compost is dry. In autumn, reduce watering to once a month. Keep plants dry in winter.

FEEDING Apply a half-strength cactus fertilizer once a month from spring to early autumn.

COMPOST Plant in cactus compost, or a 50:50 mix of loam-based (John Innes No. 2) compost and 4mm grit.

FLOWERING Give plants sufficient light and a little fertilizer.

PROPAGATION Sow seed.

COMMON PROBLEMS These plants will rot in wet compost. Pests to look out for include mealybugs and spider mites.

OROYA PERUVIANA
syn. *Echinocactus peruvianus*

One of the most popular *Oroya* and among the easiest to grow, this spiny cactus looks a little like a bird's nest. The bright green or blue-green stems, which are globe-shaped when young but eventually grow to form short columns, are covered with a tangle of long, curved, straw-coloured and reddish-brown spines. Clusters of pink or orange-red flowers are produced, even on young plants, from spring to summer.

HEIGHT & SPREAD Up to 25 x 15cm (10 x 6in).

CARE NOTES See left.

CAUTION Wear cactus gloves when handling this plant.

PARODIA

Easy to grow and generally quite small in size, *Parodia* are perfect plants for beginners. This group includes about 50 species, ranging in shape from little globes to tall cylindrical columns. The ribbed and spiny stems are topped with single flowers in spring, which may be yellow, orange, or red, although some hybrids offer other colours. The stems of some species multiply to form clusters, while others are solitary.

TEMPERATURE 10–30°C (50–86°F).

LIGHT Position in full sun; provide light shade in midsummer.

WATERING From mid-spring to late summer, water when the top 1cm (½in) of compost is dry. Reduce watering at other times, and keep plants almost dry in winter, misting them occasionally on warm days in late winter.

FEEDING Apply a half-strength cactus fertilizer once a month from mid-spring to late summer.

COMPOST Plant in cactus compost, or a 50:50 mix of loam-based (John Innes No. 2) compost and 4mm grit.

FLOWERING Flowers appear on mature plants when light levels are high enough.

PROPAGATION Sow seed or take offsets or cuttings.

COMMON PROBLEMS These plants will rot in wet compost. Check regularly for mealybugs and spider mites.

PARODIA CHRYSACANTHION AGM

syn. *Echinocactus chrysacanthion*
Golden powder puff

You can see at first glance how this little cactus gets its common name. Covered in long, fine, hair-like spines, the small round stems look exactly like golden powder puffs, although the plant is more prickly than it looks, so take care and wear gloves when handling it. In spring, a cluster of golden flowers emerges from the woolly area at the top of the plant.

HEIGHT & SPREAD Each stem grows up to 12 x 10cm (5 x 4in).

CARE NOTES See left.

CAUTION Wear cactus gloves when handling this plant.

PARODIA LENINGHAUSII AGM

syn. *Echinocactus leninghausii;
Eriocactus leninghausii;
Notocactus leninghausii*
Yellow tower cactus

The tall, candle-like stems of the yellow tower cactus are covered with soft, harmless golden spines, making it ideal for homes with children or pets. The ribbed, furry-looking stems branch and multiply from the base to form small clusters. Groups of sunny yellow flowers develop at the top of mature plants, usually when the stems reach 20cm (8in) or more in height, creating a bouquet of bright colourful blooms.

HEIGHT & SPREAD Each stem grows up to 60 x 12cm (24 x 5in).

CARE NOTES See left.

CAUTION Wear cactus gloves when handling this plant.

PARODIA SCOPA subsp. SCOPA AGM

syn. Cereus scopa;
Echinocactus scopa;
Echinopsis scopa;
Notocactus scopa;
Parodia scopa
Silver ball

The striking globes of young silver balls are covered with white woolly areas and dense, fine white or pale brown spines that shimmer in the sunlight. The spiny ribs form beautiful striped or spiralling patterns on the stems, which become more column-shaped as they age. Bright yellow flowers are produced in a ring from a woolly area on the top of the plant, producing an eye-catching combination of stem and blooms.

HEIGHT & SPREAD Each stem grows up to 50 x 15cm (20 x 6in).

CARE NOTES See opposite.

CAUTION Wear cactus gloves when handling this plant.

PARODIA MAGNIFICA AGM

syn. Eriocactus magnificus;
Notocactus magnificus
Green ball cactus;
Balloon cactus

The dramatic stems of the green ball cactus feature deep ribs edged with rows of fine yellow spines that form a graphic pattern of vertical stripes around the plant. Initially globe-shaped, the stems of older plants form short columns, and they soon multiply to create small clusters. Vibrant yellow flowers appear at the top of each stem, and mature plants may produce a few flushes throughout summer.

HEIGHT & SPREAD Each stem grows up to 30 x 15cm (12 x 6in).

CARE NOTES See opposite.

CAUTION Wear cactus gloves when handling this plant.

PARODIA SUBTERRANEA

syn. Notocactus occultus;
Parodia maassii var. *subterranean*
Underground parodia

Seek out the underground parodia for its unusual flat-topped, globe- or column-shaped stems, which in the wild grow mostly beneath the soil surface to protect them from harsh sun and wind. The ribs often spiral around the plant and feature short, claw-like brown spines surrounded by finer white bristles. Flowers appear in summer from a woolly area at the top of the stem and are usually red, although on some plants they may be bright orange or purple.

HEIGHT & SPREAD Each stem grows up to 45 x 10cm (18 x 4in).

CARE NOTES See opposite.

CAUTION Wear cactus gloves when handling this plant.

PILOSOCEREUS

Often sporting decorative blue spiny branched stems, *Pilosocereus* are shrubby or tree-like cacti that can grow up to 10m (33ft) in their native Brazil. They produce long spines along their ribbed stems, and tubular flowers in summer. Although this group of cacti includes a few species, only *Pilosocereus pachycladus* (see right) is commonly available as a house plant.

TEMPERATURE 12–30°C (54–86°F).

LIGHT Position in full sun.

WATERING During the spring and summer, water when the top 2cm (¾in) of compost is dry. In autumn, reduce watering to once a month. Keep plants dry in winter.

FEEDING Apply a half-strength cactus fertilizer once a month from spring to late summer.

COMPOST Plant in cactus compost, or a 50:50 mix of loam-based (John Innes No. 2) compost and 4mm grit.

FLOWERING Flowers appear only on mature plants that are 1m (3ft) or more in height.

PROPAGATION Sow seed or take offsets.

COMMON PROBLEMS These plants will rot in wet compost. Pests to look out for include mealybugs and spider mites.

PILOSOCEREUS PACHYCLADUS

syn. *Pilosocerus azureus;*
Pseudopilocereus pachycladus;
Pseudopilocereus pernambucoensis
Blue torch cactus

If you are looking for a desert cactus that conjures up images of old cowboy films, the blue torch cactus is the one for you. The cylindrical stems are a vivid sky blue and topped with soft tufts of orange-white hair. Short yellow spines fringe the edges of the ribs and the plant will eventually become tall and branched, creating a classic cactus silhouette. Even without the large, night-opening white or red flowers, which appear from the hairy tops on mature plants in summer, this stunning cactus is a real show-stopper. It is a large species, so ensure you have space to accommodate it before buying.

HEIGHT & SPREAD Each stem grows up to 1m x 15cm (3ft x 6in).

CARE NOTES See left.

CAUTION Wear cactus gloves when handling this plant.

PYGMAEOCEREUS

These tiny cacti produce clumps of short cylindrical stems. The ribs in some species may spiral around the stem, and they are covered with soft spines. Cactus-lovers grow *Pygmeaocereus* for their night-opening, scented, usually white flowers, which look like fireworks shooting out from the sides of the stems on long tubes.

TEMPERATURE 5–30°C (41–86°F).

LIGHT Position in full sun and light shade in midsummer.

WATERING During the spring and summer, water when the top 2cm (¾in) of compost is dry. In autumn, reduce watering, and keep plants dry in winter when dormant. Provide good ventilation in summer.

FEEDING Apply a half-strength cactus fertilizer once in late spring.

COMPOST Plant in cactus compost, or a 50:50 mix of loam-based (John Innes No. 2) compost and 4mm grit.

FLOWERING Flowers will develop if light levels are high enough.

PROPAGATION Sow seed or take offsets.

COMMON PROBLEMS These plants will rot in wet compost. Pests to look out for include mealybugs, spider mites, scale, thrips, and aphids.

PYGMAEOCEREUS BYLESIANUS

syn. *Arthrocereus bylesianus*

The dark green stems of this little column-shaped cactus have wavy ribs and rust-coloured or grey spines. The plant's main attraction is the series of white summer flowers, each of which opens for just one night and emits an unusual scent. This cactus is more suitable for experienced growers than beginners because it requires strong sunlight and good ventilation, and mature plants are very prone to rotting if overwatered.

HEIGHT & SPREAD Each stem grows up to 8 x 2cm (3 x 1in).

CARE NOTES See opposite.

REBUTIA

With their colourful flowers and little globe-shaped, dimpled stems, these easy-to-grow cacti are perfect for beginners. Clusters of short spines, which sprout from woolly areas on the stems, give plants a spotty appearance. The flowers come in a range of colours, including white, pink, red, and yellow, and appear around the base of the stems in spring or summer, even on relatively young plants. *Rebutia* also produce large numbers of seeds that germinate freely around the parent plant.

TEMPERATURE 5–30°C (41–86°F); keep cool in winter at about 5-10°C (41–50°F).

LIGHT Position in full sun for most of the year, but provide light shade in summer.

WATERING During the spring and summer, water when the top 1cm (½in) of compost is dry. In autumn, reduce watering. Keep plants dry in winter.

FEEDING Apply a half-strength cactus fertilizer once a month from spring to late summer.

COMPOST Plant in cactus compost, or a 50:50 mix of loam-based (John Innes No. 2) compost and 4mm grit.

FLOWERING Flowers appear freely, but are more likely to develop when plants are kept cool in winter.

PROPAGATION Sow seed or take offsets.

COMMON PROBLEMS These plants will rot in wet compost. Pests to look out for include mealybugs and spider mites.

REBUTIA ARENACEA AGM

syn. *Sulcorebutia arenacea*
Arenaceous crown cactus

A beautiful little species, the arenaceous crown cactus forms green, globe-shaped, flat-topped stems decorated with a symmetrical swirling pattern of pale yellow and orange spines. As plants mature, they develop into attractive clumps, and in spring, clusters of yellowish-orange flowers appear around the base of the stems.

HEIGHT & SPREAD Each stem grows up to 4 x 6cm (1½ x 2½in).

CARE NOTES See left.

CAUTION Wear cactus gloves when handling this plant.

REBUTIA 'CARNIVAL'

syn. *Aylostera* 'Carnival';
Sulcorebutia 'Carnival'
Carnival crown cactus

Popular for their brightly coloured flowers, the carnival crown cactus is a group of hybrids that produce red, pink, white, and orange flowers – some may be bicoloured. The small globe-shaped stems become more cylindrical with age, and feature a dense covering of short white or sandy-coloured spines. The blooms appear in spring.

HEIGHT & SPREAD Each stem grows up to 4 x 6cm (1½ x 2½in).

CARE NOTES See p113.

CAUTION Wear cactus gloves when handling this plant.

REBUTIA FLAVISTYLA

syn. *Aylostera flavistyla*
Flame crown cactus

For a week in spring, an explosion of bright orange, daisy-like flowers almost cover the tiny body of the flame crown cactus. Deservedly popular, the dimpled, globe-shaped stems feature short, glassy-white spines that are soft to the touch and look like hair.

HEIGHT & SPREAD Up to 5 x 5cm (2 x 2in).

CARE NOTES See p113.

CAUTION Wear cactus gloves when handling this plant.

REBUTIA HELIOSA

syn. *Aylostera heliosa*
Heliosa crown cactus

The large daisy-like orange flowers of the heliosa crown cactus make a dramatic focal point when they appear in spring, smothering the tiny spherical or short cylindrical stems so that the plant looks like a tiny florist's bouquet. This cactus is covered with short brown and white fine, hair-like spines and the stems quickly make small clumps.

HEIGHT & SPREAD Clumps grow up to 4 x 10cm (1½ x 4in).

CARE NOTES See p113.

REBUTIA HELIOSA x ALBIFLORA
syn. *Aylostera heliosa*
White heliosa crown cactus

A good choice for those who find the orange flowers of the heliosa crown cactus a little too bright and brash, this plant has similar stems, but more subtle cream-coloured flowers with pale pink streaks. You may find this plant labelled *Rebutia heliosa* 'Sunrise'.

HEIGHT & SPREAD Clumps grow up to 4 x 10cm (1½ x 4in).

CARE NOTES See p113.

CAUTION Wear cactus gloves when handling this plant.

REBUTIA MINISCULA 'KRAINZIANA' AGM
syn. *Rebutia krainziana*
Krainziana crown cactus

Loved for its dark green dimpled stems and a neat spotty pattern of white spines that are soft to the touch, the Krainziana crown cactus also produces a striking display of daisy-like flowers in early spring. Because it has some natural variation, you may see this little cactus with bright red, orange, yellow, or white blooms.

HEIGHT & SPREAD Each stem grows up to 7 x 10cm (2¾ x 4in).

CARE NOTES See p113.

CAUTION Wear cactus gloves when handling this plant.

REBUTIA
SENILIS AGM

syn. *Rebutia senilis* var. *senilis*
Fire crown cactus

Clusters of tiny flat-topped, globe-shaped stems covered with long, glassy-white bristly spines form a backdrop to the fire crown cactus' large flowers, which are its star attraction when they appear in spring. The blooms are usually orange or crimson, but can be white, red, or yellow.

HEIGHT & SPREAD Each stem grows up to 7 x 7cm (2¾ x 2¾in).

CARE NOTES See p113.

CAUTION Wear cactus gloves when handling this plant.

REBUTIA
VIOLACIFLORA

syn. *Rebutia minuscula* subsp. *violaciflora*;
Rebutia minuscula f. *violaciflora*
Violet crown cactus

Bristly yellow or tan spines, which are longer than those found growing on many *Rebutia* species, create a pattern of starry clusters over the violet crown cactus' tiny globe-shaped stems. The plant gets its name from the colour of the funnel-shaped spring flowers, which are a delicate pale violet.

HEIGHT & SPREAD Up to 2 x 4cm (¾ x 1½in).

CARE NOTES See p113.

RHIPSALIS

Not immediately recognizable as cacti, *Rhipsalis* are from the tropical rainforests of South America, the Caribbean, and Central America. They are epiphytic, which means they grow on trees, and most species have long, trailing, or sprawling spineless stems that are best displayed in a large hanging basket. They also prefer shade, unlike their desert-dwelling cousins. Some plants have cylindrical stems that hang down like green hair, while others are flattened ribbons, and a few feature bristles or spines. The small flowers are usually white, although some have yellow or red blooms. These develop along the length of the stems in winter or early spring, and are followed by inedible white berries.

TEMPERATURE 10–30°C (50–86°F).

LIGHT Position in light shade out of direct sun.

WATERING During the spring and summer, water well when the top of compost is just dry. In autumn and winter, reduce watering but do not let plants dry out completely. Mist stems regularly to raise humidity levels.

FEEDING Apply a balanced fertilizer once a month from spring to early autumn.

COMPOST Plant in orchid compost.

FLOWERING These plants bloom profusely if grown in an even, high temperature and shade. They will drop their buds if plants are moved.

PROPAGATION Take stem cuttings.

COMMON PROBLEMS Plants are generally pest-free.

RHIPSALIS BACCIFERA

syn. *Cassytha baccifera;*
Rhipsalis baccifera subsp. *baccifera;*
Rhipsalis cassytha
Mistletoe cactus; Spaghetti cactus

Named after its inedible white spring berries, which look like mistletoe, this cactus' other common name describes its green spaghetti-like branched stems. These flowing stems will trail elegantly from a hanging basket and can reach over 1m (3ft) in length, so hang the plant up high enough to allow them space to develop. Creamy-white flowers form at the stem tips and precede the berries.

HEIGHT & SPREAD Up to 1.5 x 0.6m (5 x 2ft).

CARE NOTES See opposite.

RHIPSALIS CEREUSCULA

syn. *Erythrorhipsalis cereuscula;*
Hariota cereuscula
Coral cactus;
Rice cactus

This unusual cactus looks like a mound of green coral, hence its common name. Perfect for a tall pot or hanging basket, the cyclindrical stems are armed with soft, bristly spines, and branch out at the tips. In late winter or spring, tiny creamy-white blooms that look like snowflakes develop at the stem tips.

HEIGHT & SPREAD Up to 60 x 60cm (24 x 24in).

CARE NOTES See opposite.

RHIPSALIS MONACANTHA AGM

syn. *Acanthorhipsalis monacantha;*
Hariota monacantha;
Pfeiffera monacantha
One-spined wickerware cactus

Unlike most *Rhipsalis,* the one-spined wickerware cactus features sharp black spines and white bristles along the edges of its ribbon-like, serrated stems. In late winter or spring, small orange bell-shaped flowers develop next to the black spines, often blooming for a few months. Stems may turn red if the plant becomes stressed due to poor care.

HEIGHT & SPREAD Up to 20 x 45cm (8 x 18in).

CARE NOTES See p116.

CAUTION Wear cactus gloves when handling this plant.

RHIPSALIS MICRANTHA

An elegant *Rhipsalis,* ideal for a large basket, this tropical cactus produces flowing green ribbon-like stems with wavy margins. Grow it where you can appreciate the small white flowers that appear along the stem margins in late winter, and the inedible white berries that follow in spring and summer.

HEIGHT & SPREAD Up to 0.6 x 1m (2 x 3ft).

CARE NOTES See p116.

RHIPSALIS PACHYPTERA
syn. *Hariota pachyptera*

The trailing, flattened stems of this beautiful plant are divided into large leaf-shaped, spineless segments. The segments' lobed edges add a decorative touch to the stems, and they are sometimes also tinged with red. Creamy-yellow or whitish scented flowers form along the edges of the stems, opening from pink buds, which are also attractive. The blooms are followed by inedible round white berries.

HEIGHT & SPREAD Up to 1.5 x 0.6m (5 x 2ft).

CARE NOTES See p116.

RHIPSALIS PILOCARPA
syn. *Erythrorhipsalis pilocarpa*
Hairy-fruited wickerware cactus

With its unusual spaghetti-like stems, which are covered with soft hairs and tipped with fine bristles, this cactus makes for a great talking point. White scented flowers appear in winter or early spring, followed by inedible red berries.

HEIGHT & SPREAD Up to 0.6 x 1m (2 x 3ft).

CARE NOTES See p116.

SCHLUMBERGERA

This small group of tropical cacti comprises about nine species, but only two – *Schlumbergera* x *buckleyi* and *Schlumbergera truncata* - are widely available and both are known commonly as Christmas cacti. These plants are epiphytes, and cling to trees in the rainforests of their native Brazil. They produce fountains of trailing stems, which are divided into leaf-like segments, and are grown primarily for their brightly coloured winter flowers.

TEMPERATURE 12-24°C (55-75°F); reduce the temperature to 12-15°C (55-59°F) after flowering and again in autumn.

LIGHT Position in light shade out of direct sun.

WATERING In summer and late winter, water well when the surface of the compost is just dry. After flowering, keep the compost almost dry, then resume watering more frequently in summer. Reduce watering again just before the flower buds form in autumn, but water more frequently again as soon as you see them developing. Mist stems regularly to raise humidity levels.

FEEDING Apply a balanced liquid fertilizer once a month from spring to early autumn.

COMPOST Plant in orchid compost.

FLOWERING These plants bloom easily but are likely to drop their buds if they are moved at this stage.

PROPAGATION Sow seed or take stem cuttings.

COMMON PROBLEMS Plants are generally pest-free, but check them occasionally for mealybugs.

SCHLUMBERGERA x BUCKLEYI AGM

syn. *Epiphyllum* x *buckleyi*
Christmas cactus

Prized for its beautiful pink pendent winter flowers, the blooms of the Christmas cactus look like those of a fuchsia and open during the festive season, hence its common name. The flowers appear at the tips of the glossy green stems, which are divided into scallop-edged segments and create a mound of trailing lush green growth throughout the year.

HEIGHT & SPREAD Up to 45 x 45cm (18 x 18in).

CARE NOTES See left.

SCHLUMBERGERA TRUNCATA

syn. *Schlumbergera* x *bridgesii;*
Epiphyllum truncatum var. *bridgesii*
Christmas cactus

Almost identical to *Schlumbergera* x *buckleyi,* the stem segments of this Christmas cactus have toothed rather than scalloped edges. In all other respects it looks the same as its close cousin. You may find hybrids of this species with purple, orange, white, or multicoloured flowers.

HEIGHT & SPREAD Up to 45 x 45cm (18 x 18in).

CARE NOTES See opposite.

STENOCACTUS

These small, globe-shaped, easy-to-grow cacti are perfect for beginners. They flower profusely and make a pretty display on a narrow windowsill when their white blooms appear in early spring. Another attractive feature of some species is their unusual pleated ribs, which makes them look like little round corals. The sparse spines are often long and produced in starry clusters.

TEMPERATURE 5–30°C (41–86°F)

LIGHT Position in full sun for most of the year, but provide some shade in summer.

WATERING During the spring and summer, water when the top 1cm (½in) of compost is dry. In autumn, reduce watering to once a month. Keep plants dry in winter.

FEEDING Apply a half-strength cactus fertilizer once a month from late spring to late summer.

COMPOST Plant in cactus compost, or a 50:50 mix of loam-based (John Innes No. 2) compost and 4mm grit.

FLOWERING Flowers appear freely on mature plants, given sufficient light and a little fertilizer.

PROPAGATION Sow seed or take offsets.

COMMON PROBLEMS These plants will rot in wet compost. Pests to look out for include mealybugs and spider mites.

STENOCACTUS MULTICOSTATUS AGM

syn. *Echinocactus multicostatus;*
Echinofossulocactus multicostatus
Wave cactus;
Brain cactus

It may be tiny, but the wave cactus has many beautiful features that make up for its diminutive size. Long, curved, cream-coloured spines and short white spines form clusters on spiralling pleated ribs, and in some plants, the flattened globes are also topped by red spines. The flowers appear in spring from the crown of the plant and can be white, pinkish-purple, or violet, with a darker violet to purple stripe.

HEIGHT & SPREAD Each stem grows up to 12 x 15cm (5 x 6in).

CARE NOTES See left.

CAUTION Wear cactus gloves when handling this plant.

STENOCEREUS

Column-shaped or tree-like, these sharp-spined cacti can grow into towering plants, though they will remain slightly smaller when restricted to a pot indoors. Make sure you have a large area to show them off, not least because the sharp spines on the stems need a space where they will not cause injury. The flowers develop near the top of the plant and are mostly nocturnal. *Stenocereus* are easy to grow and also produce edible fruits.

TEMPERATURE 5–30°C (41–86°F); keep cool at 8–12°C (46–54°F) in winter.

LIGHT Position in full sun, but provide some shade in summer.

WATERING During the spring and summer, water when the top 2cm (¾in) of compost is dry. In autumn, reduce watering to once a month. Keep plants dry in winter.

FEEDING Apply a half-strength cactus fertilizer from spring to late summer.

COMPOST Plant in cactus compost, or a 50:50 mix of loam-based (John Innes No. 2) compost and 4mm grit.

FLOWERING Keep plants cool in winter to encourage blooms to form.

PROPAGATION Sow seed or take cuttings.

COMMON PROBLEMS These plants will rot in wet compost. Check plants regularly for mealybugs, scale insects, and spider mites.

STENOCEREUS THURBERI

syn. *Cereus thurberi;*
Pilocereus thurberi
Organ pipe cactus

As the name suggests, the stems of the organ pipe cactus form tall, slim, spiny columns, and mature plants also branch out from the base. The white to pale lilac flowers, which appear in flushes from spring to late summer, open for one night and the following day before withering. The spiny, sweet, edible fruits, known as "pitahaya", are more prized than the blooms in their native Mexico.

HEIGHT & SPREAD Up to 1.5 x 0.15m (5ft x 6in).

CARE NOTES See left.

CAUTION Wear gloves when handling this plant.

SULCOREBUTIA

These small cacti produce globe-shape stems that slowly multiply to form clusters. A few species have dramatic purple or red stems, and while some *Sulcorebutia* are spiny, others have very short, almost imperceptible spines. The spring flowers come in a range of bright colours, including pink and yellow, and develop at the base of the stem.

TEMPERATURE 5–30°C (41–86°F); plants prefer a cool spot at 5–10°C (42–50°F) in winter, and may survive -5°C (23°F) for short spells in dry soil.

LIGHT Position in full sun for most of the year, but provide young plants with light shade. All *Sulcorebutia* need some shade in summer too.

WATERING During the spring and summer, water when the top 1cm (½in) of compost is dry. In autumn, reduce watering to once a month, and keep plants dry in winter.

FEEDING Apply a half-strength cactus fertilizer once a month from late spring to late summer.

COMPOST Plant in cactus compost, or a 50:50 mix of loam based (John Innes No. 2) compost and 4mm grit.

FLOWERING Keep plants cool in winter, and give sufficient light and a little fertilizer to encourage flowering.

PROPAGATION Sow seed or take offsets.

COMMON PROBLEMS These plants will rot in wet compost. Pests to look out for include mealybugs, scale insects, and spider mites.

SULCOREBUTIA LANGERI
syn. *Rebutia cardenasiana*

You may find this little cactus classified as a *Sulcorebutia langeri* or *Rebutia cardenasiana*, so check for both names when searching for it. It is prized for its clusters of tiny dark green globes covered with feathery white spines that create a lacy effect and are soft to the touch. Its sunny yellow daisy-like flowers are often larger than the stems, and appear in spring.

HEIGHT & SPREAD Up to 8 x 15cm (3 x 6in).

CARE NOTES See left.

SULCOREBUTIA RAUSCHII

syn. *Rebutia canigueralii* subsp. *rauschii*;
Rebutia rauschii f. *violacidermis*;
Sulcorebutia rauschii f. *violacidermis*

The beautiful purple and green dimpled stems of this clustering species make it stand out, despite its miniature size. The stems also feature short, black spines that are flattened against the surface in a fishbone pattern. As a bonus, eye-catching magenta-pink flowers appear in late spring, adding to this tiny plant's charms.

HEIGHT & SPREAD Up to 2 x 3cm (¾ x 1in).

CARE NOTES See p123.

THELOCACTUS

Small and spiny, these little globe-shaped cacti often grow to form short cylindrical stems. All species are easy to grow and ideal for beginners, but most are heavily armoured with sharp spines, so display them out of reach of children and pets. Some *Thelocactus* have defined ribs – a few form a spiral pattern – while the stems of others are more unusual, featuring raised areas (known as "tubercles") that divide the surface into hexagonal pillow-like segments. The flowers are funnel-shaped and come in yellow, red, or purple. The blooms develop at the top of the plant and can appear from late winter to late summer.

TEMPERATURE 5–30°C (41–86°F); can tolerate -5°C (23°F) if the soil is dry.

LIGHT Position in full sun, but provide a little shade in midsummer.

WATERING During the spring and summer, water when the top 2cm (¾in) of compost is dry. In autumn, reduce watering to once a month. Keep plants dry in winter. Provide good air circulation to reduce the risk of rot.

FEEDING Apply a half-strength cactus fertilizer once a month from late spring to late summer.

COMPOST Plant in cactus compost, or a 50:50 mix of loam-based (John Innes No. 2) compost and 4mm grit.

FLOWERING Flowers appear on mature plants grown in good light and given a little fertilizer.

PROPAGATION Sow seed.

COMMON PROBLEMS These plants are prone to rotting in wet compost. Check plants regularly for mealybugs, scale insects, and spider mites.

THELOCACTUS BICOLOR AGM

syn. *Echinocactus bicolor*;
Ferocactus bicolor
Glory of Texas

A forest of long, sharp, straw-coloured spines radiates out from the ribs of this popular species, making a striking contrast with the green stems beneath. Plants may be globe-shaped when young but will eventually form short columns. The magenta flowers with red throats open from spring to autumn.

HEIGHT & SPREAD UP Each stems grows up to 20 x 10cm (8 x 4in).

CARE NOTES See left.

CAUTION Wear gloves when handling this plant.

THELOCACTUS MACDOWELLII AGM

syn. *Echinocactus macdowellii;*
Thelocactus conothelos var. *macdowellii*

A prickly coat of long, glassy-white, sharp spines wrap around this small globe-shaped cactus, giving a clear signal that it should be handled with care. The winter flowers are pink with a yellow centre, and emerge from clusters of dark pink buds that push out from between the fierce spines in spring. Some plants may bloom again later in the year.

HEIGHT & SPREAD UP Each stem grows up to 10 x 10cm (4 x 4in).

CARE NOTES See opposite.

CAUTION Wear gloves when handling this plant.

THELOCACTUS HEXAEDROPHORUS AGM

syn. *Echinocactus hexaedrophorus;*
Thelomastus hexaedrophorus

It may be small, but this plant's striking good looks make it very collectable. The olive-green or greyish-green stems feature raised hexagonal segments, which can be tinged with pink or purple when the plant is grown in strong light. Star-shaped clusters of long, curved, reddish-brown spines shoot out from the centre of each segment, while the elegant silvery-white flowers have a pale pink central stripe and appear at the top of the plant.

HEIGHT & SPREAD Each stem grows up to 7 x 15cm (3½ x 6in).

CARE NOTES See opposite.

CAUTION Wear gloves when handling this plant.

SUCCULENTS

As a horticultural term, "succulent" describes a range of different plant types, including some that may surprise first-time collectors, such as *Hoya* (see p165) and *Sansevieria* (see p176). As house plants, succulents are grown primarily for their striking foliage, which comes in a range of shapes and colours. If well cared for, however, many succulents can also be encouraged to flower, providing an added burst of colour. While succulents are generally easy to care for, they can suffer if they do not receive plenty of light, or if they are overwatered.

ADROMISCHUS

With a wide range of unusual leaf shapes to choose from, these succulents make up for their small size with their beautiful colours and varied textures. Some have bright green flattened leaves, others are grey and look more like pebbles or shells, while a few resemble ravioli with crimped edges. Tiny star-shaped flowers are produced on long stems in late spring or summer. However, some people remove the blooms because their nectar can encourage fungal diseases.

TEMPERATURE 5–30°C (41–86°F)

LIGHT Position in bright light out of direct sun.

WATERING From spring to early autumn, water when the top of the compost is dry. Reduce watering in autumn and winter so that the compost is just moist and the leaves do not shrivel.

FEEDING Apply a half-strength cactus fertilizer once a month from spring to late summer.

COMPOST Plant in cactus compost, or a 50:50 mix of loam-based (John Innes No. 2) compost and 4mm grit.

FLOWERING Plants will flower without any special treatment.

PROPAGATION Take leaf or stem cuttings.

COMMON PROBLEMS Plants are prone to rot if grown in wet compost. Check regularly for mealybugs. Remove faded blooms to reduce the risk of them falling onto the compost and rotting, which will encourage fungal diseases.

ADROMISCHUS TRIGYNUS
syn. *Adromischus rupicola*
Calico hearts

Grow this tiny succulent for its elegant flat, paddle-shaped, grey-green leaves with dark purple-brown speckles, which develop around the central stem. It rarely flowers indoors, but since the yellow–green blooms are not considered to be as interesting as the foliage, they are not missed.

HEIGHT AND SPREAD Up to 15 x 15cm (6 x 6in).

CARE NOTES See opposite.

ADROMISCHUS COOPERI AGM
Plover eggs

This succulent takes its name from the dark purple spots that cover its green leaves, rather than the shape of its foliage, which actually resembles a tiny tube of toothpaste. Like most *Adromischus*, this beautiful species is a good choice for those without full sun, as a little shade helps it to maintain its decorative markings. Small pink flowers appear in summer on tall stems that shoot out from the middle of the plant.

HEIGHT AND SPREAD Up to 7 x 15cm (3 x 6in).

CARE NOTES See opposite.

AEONIUM

Admired for their decorative foliage, this group includes tall dramatic plants with woody stems topped with rosettes of fleshy leaves, and smaller, more subtle species, featuring flatter rosettes. All produce small, star-shaped flowers on long stems from late winter to summer. After blooming the flowering rosettes will die, but they usually produce offsets (new shoots) that will grow on to take their place, or you can take cuttings to propagate new plants (see p203). Many *Aeonium* species become semi-dormant during very hot summers but their foliage will not wither if plants are grown outside in light shade.

TEMPERATURE 10–24°C (50–75°F).

LIGHT Position in full sun but provide some shade in summer.

WATERING From autumn to late spring, water when the top 1cm (½in) of compost feels dry; reduce in summer when plants may become semi-dormant. Grow outside in summer after the frosts to increase humidity around plants.

FEEDING Apply a half-strength balanced liquid fertilizer once a month in the growing season from winter to late spring.

COMPOST Plant in cactus compost, or a 50:50 mix of loam-based (John Innes No. 2) compost and 4mm grit.

FLOWERING Plants will flower in spring if fed and watered regularly; young plants may not flower for a few years.

PROPAGATION Sow seed or take cuttings in early spring.

COMMON PROBLEMS Plants are susceptible to root rot if overwatered or left sitting in wet compost. Check plants regularly for mealybugs.

AEONIUM ARBOREUM 'ATROPURPUREUM'

syn. *Aeonium arboreum* var. *atropurpureum*
Dark purple houseleek tree

Mature dark purple houseleek trees form a striking silhouette, their tall branched stems resembling a candelabra holding leafy rosettes. Conical clusters of starry yellow flowers rise up from the rosettes in late spring.

HEIGHT AND SPREAD
Up to 1.5 x 0.9m (5 x 3ft).

CARE NOTES See left.

AEONIUM | PLANT PROFILES

AEONIUM CANARIENSE var. SUBPLANUM

syn. *Aeonium subplanum*
Canary Island flat giant houseleek

The Canary Island flat giant houseleek is not especially tall for a shrubby aeonium, but its leafy rosettes are exceptionally large, which explains the name. The glossy rounded light green leaves are tinged pinkish-purple in winter when temperatures are low or if the compost is dry, creating an eye-catching two-tone effect. Yellow flower spikes emerge from the centre of the leaf rosettes in spring.

HEIGHT AND SPREAD Up to 50 x 40cm (20 x 16in).

CARE NOTES See opposite.

AEONIUM 'BLUSHING BEAUTY' AGM

Blushing Beauty houseleek tree

A sought-after, colourful hybrid, 'Blushing Beauty' is similar in structure to *Aeonium arboreum* (see opposite) but forms a more compact plant. Its green leaf rosettes are tinged with reddish-pink, and large clusters of tiny yellow flowers appear in spring and summer.

HEIGHT AND SPREAD Up to 70 x 60cm (28 x 24in).

CARE NOTES See opposite.

AEONIUM DECORUM

Green pinwheel

The bright colours of the green pinwheel aeonium will shine out when grouped together with dark-leaved or plain green plants. The sturdy stems hold rosettes of pale green oval leaves with orange-red and red margins, which become brighter when the plant is grown in full sun. Soft pink starry flowers appear in spring. Also look out for *Aeonium decorum* var. *guarimiarense*, which has green leaves with red tips.

HEIGHT AND SPREAD Up to 60 x 50cm (24 x 20in).

CARE NOTES See opposite.

AEONIUM | PLANT PROFILES

AEONIUM HAWORTHII AGM
Haworth's pinwheel

An elegant and sought-after species, the branched stems of Haworth's pinwheel are topped with rosettes of large, bluish-green leaves, often with red-tinged margins. The flowers, which appear in late spring, are pale creamy yellow, and they too may be tinged pink.

HEIGHT AND SPREAD Up to 60 x 60cm (24 x 24in).

CARE NOTES See p128.

AEONIUM TABULIFORME AGM
syn. *Aeonium berthelotianum; Aeonium macrolepum*
Flat-topped aeonium; Dinner plate aeonium

The flat-topped aeonium looks quite different from its shrubby, branching cousins. The ground-hugging, flat rosettes – made up of tightly packed, overlapping light green leaves – can reach dinner-plate proportions, hence its common name. Small starry yellow flowers appear on tall stems from the centre of the rosettes in spring. Grow it in a shallow pot in a bright room, such as a conservatory, turning it regularly to encourage even growth.

HEIGHT AND SPREAD Up to 10 x 30cm (4 x 12in).

CARE NOTES See p128.

AEONIUM 'ZWARTKOP' AGM
syn. *Aeonium arboreum* 'Zwartkop'
'Zwartkop' houseleek tree;
Black aeonium

Similar to *Aeonium arboreum* 'Atropurpureum' (see pp128), the dark burgundy leaf rosettes of this houseleek tree are almost black, with a bright green centre. It is a highly prized cultivar and best grown with more colourful species or a plain green variety that will show up its contrasting hue. In winter, bright yellow flowers create a dazzling combination with the dark foliage.

HEIGHT AND SPREAD Up to 60 x 60cm (24 x 24in).

CARE NOTES See p128.

AEONIUM 'VELOUR'
syn. *Aeonium arboreum* 'Velour'
Velour houseleek tree

A show-stopping *Aeonium* that is guaranteed to turn heads, this plant is coveted for its green-centred, dark purple leafy rosettes, which have a soft, velvety appearance. As the plant matures, more rosettes form on the branched stems, producing a striking effect. Yellow flowers appear in early spring.

HEIGHT AND SPREAD Up to 60 x 50cm (24 x 20in).

CARE NOTES See p128.

AGAVE

Spiky leaves and dramatic silhouettes make the plants in this group deservedly popular in both homes and gardens. They form a rosette of thick, fleshy leaves, which, in many species, are tipped with a sharp spine. *Agave* are grown primarily for their foliage, which can be all shades of green or variegated with yellow or cream stripes. Flowers are rarely produced on house plants, but the nectar of those grown outside is used as an alternative sweetener to sugar. Smaller varieties or young plants are the best choices for a house plant collection, as the mature plants of many species are too big for most homes.

TEMPERATURE -5–30°C (23–86°F); can tolerate freezing conditions if the soil is dry.

LIGHT Position in full sun; place in light shade in summer.

WATERING During the spring and summer, water when the top 2cm (¾in) of compost is dry. In autumn and winter keep the compost almost dry, watering just enough to prevent the leaves shrivelling.

FEEDING Apply a half-strength liquid fertilizer once a month during late spring and summer.

COMPOST Plant in cactus compost, or a 50:50 mix of loam-based (John Innes No. 2) compost and 4mm grit.

FLOWERING Flowers rarely appear on house plants.

PROPAGATION Sow seed or take offsets.

COMMON PROBLEMS These plants will rot in wet compost. Pests to look out for include scale insects and mealybugs.

AGAVE AMERICANA 'MEDIOPICTA ALBA' AGM

syn. *Agave americana* f. *medio-picta alba*
American century plant

The sculptural leaves of the popular American century plant feature creamy white and bluish-grey stripes and make a dramatic statement in a large, bright room. Grown outside, it can reach up to 1m (3ft) in height and width, but remains more compact indoors in a pot. However, it still needs plenty of space if you are to avoid the sharp spines that guard the serrated edges and tips of the leaves. The yellow–green flowers will not appear on indoor-grown plants.

HEIGHT AND SPREAD Up to 1 x 1m (3 x 3ft).

CARE NOTES See left.

CAUTION Wear cactus gloves when handling this plant; the sap can also cause skin irritation.

AGAVE AMERICANA 'VARIEGATA' AGM

Variegated American century plant

This large, handsome century plant puts on a show with its yellow-edged grey–green leaves. Buy young plants to grow indoors and display where you can admire their beautiful foliage without being pricked by the spines. When these *Agave* get too big for their pots, consider planting them outside in a sunny, sheltered spot in free-draining soil, where they will survive several degrees of frost.

HEIGHT AND SPREAD Up to 1.5 x 1.5m (5 x 5ft).

CARE NOTES See left.

CAUTION Wear cactus gloves when handling this plant; the sap can also cause skin irritation.

AGAVE FILIFERA AGM
syn. *Agave filamentosa*
Thread agave

The pointed leaves of the thread agave are covered with white hairs, hence its common name. The foliage of this unusual species is also edged with thin white stripes, adding to the plant's decorative appeal. Greenish-white flowers, which form at the top of towering stems, rarely appear on plants grown indoors.

HEIGHT AND SPREAD Up to 45 x 45cm (18 x 18in).

CARE NOTES See opposite.

CAUTION Wear cactus gloves when handling this plant; the sap can also cause skin irritation.

AGAVE COLORATA
Mescal ceniza

The colourful wavy-edged leaves of the mescal ceniza, together with its relatively small size, account for this plant's popularity. The beautiful frosty grey-blue or light grey leaves are armed with vicious spines, so make sure it has enough space to avoid injury. The flowers are red in bud, and yellow and orange when in bloom.

HEIGHT AND SPREAD Up to 1.2 x 1.2m (4 x 4ft).

CARE NOTES See opposite.

CAUTION Wear cactus gloves when handling this plant; the sap can also cause skin irritation.

AGAVE PARRASANA AGM

syn. *Agave wislizenii*
Cabbage head agave

One of the smaller species, the cabbage head agave is perfect for a windowsill succulent collection when young. Its short, wide leaves are pale blue-green with thorny, toothed edges and a waxy coating. These plants are spiky, so take care when handling them. Flowers are red in bud, then yellow when open.

HEIGHT AND SPREAD Up to 60 x 60cm (2 x2ft).

CARE NOTES See p132.

CAUTION Wear cactus gloves when handling this plant; the sap can also cause skin irritation.

AGAVE PARRASANA 'FIREBALL'
Variegated cabbage head agave

A rare cultivar of the popular cabbage head agave (see left), 'Fireball' differs from its parent only in the colour of the leaves, which are blue-grey with thin creamy yellow margins. When backlit, these margins make the foliage look as if it is on fire.

HEIGHT AND SPREAD Up to 60 x 60cm (2 x2ft).

CARE NOTES See p132.

CAUTION Wear cactus gloves when handling this plant; the sap can also cause skin irritation.

AGAVE PARRYI AGM
Parry's agave; Mescal agave

The winning feature of the Parry's agave is its elegant silvery grey-blue foliage, which is tipped and edged with short dark spines. Yellow flowers, tinged red or pink in bud, appear on mature plants grown outside, but are unlikely to develop on house plants.

HEIGHT AND SPREAD Up to 60 x 80cm (24 x 32in).

CARE NOTES See p132.

CAUTION Wear cactus gloves when handling this plant; the sap can also cause skin irritation.

AGAVE PARRYI subsp. NEOMEXICANA
syn. *Agave neomexicana*
New Mexico agave

The New Mexico agave produces upright rosettes of narrow blue-green to powder blue leaves, armed with dark burgundy spines along the edges. Golden yellow flowers on long stems may appear if the plant is grown outside in summer.

HEIGHT AND SPREAD 45 x 60cm (18 x 24in).

CARE NOTES See p132.

CAUTION Wear cactus gloves when handling this plant; the sap can also cause skin irritation.

AGAVE VICTORIAE-REGINAE AGM

syn. *Agave ferdinandi-regis;*
Agave scabra x *victoriae-reginae*
Queen Victoria century plant; Royal agave

The compact Queen Victoria century plant forms an eye-catching rounded rosette that looks a little like an artichoke head. The plant features three-sided, mid-green, spine-tipped leaves, with smooth, spineless edges and white or black margins. Creamy-white summer flowers may appear on long stems from the centre of the leaf rosettes of mature plants.

HEIGHT AND SPREAD Up to 30 x 30cm (12 x 12in).

CARE NOTES See p132.

AGAVE STRICTA AGM

syn. *Agave striata* subsp. *stricta*
Hedgehog agave

Unlike its cousins, the unusual hedgehog agave forms a spiky sphere of skewer-like leaves, each armed with a spine at the tip. This relatively compact *Agave* quickly forms offshoots that each produce clusters of leafy rosettes, giving it an even quirkier appearance as each plantlet develops its own ball of foliage. Small red flowers appear in summer on mature plants.

HEIGHT AND SPREAD Up to 40 x 40cm (16 x 16in).

CARE NOTES See p132.

ALBUCA

Not strictly a succulent, although succulent specialist nurseries often sell it, *Albuca* needs slightly different care to most of the other plants in this chapter. The spiralling forms are the most popular, prized for their fascinating leaves, which resemble green corkscrews. *Albuca* plants grow from a bulb, and each one produces a single central flower spike bearing nodding bell-shaped green blooms with pale yellow margins. Plants go dormant after flowering in summer but will start growing again in the autumn.

TEMPERATURE 5–30°C (41–86°F)

LIGHT Position in full sun, but provide some shade in summer.

WATERING From autumn to late spring when plants are in growth, water sparingly, applying it only when the top of the compost feels dry; plants will curl more in drier conditions. When dormant in summer, keep almost dry, then water more frequently when growth appears in the autumn.

FEEDING Apply a general-purpose granular fertilizer in autumn at half the dose recommended on the label.

COMPOST Plant in bulb compost, or a 50:50 mix of loam-based (John Innes No. 2) compost and 4mm grit.

FLOWERING Flowers appear on plants given sufficient water and a little fertilizer.

PROPAGATION Plant bulbs in autumn or divide existing plants.

COMMON PROBLEMS These plants will rot in wet compost. Few pests affect them.

ALBUCA SPIRALIS 'FRIZZLE SIZZLE'
Ornithogalum circinatum 'Frizzle Sizzle'
Corkscrew albuca 'Frizzle Sizzle'

An amazing plant not to be missed, the corkscrew albuca 'Frizzle Sizzle' has fast-growing, tightly spiralling dark green leaves. The flower spike, which shoots up through the foliage in late winter or early spring, holds dainty fragrant yellow and green nodding flowers. In summer, when dormant, the foliage will disappear below the surface.

HEIGHT AND SPREAD Up to 20 x 20cm (8 x 8in).

CARE NOTES See left.

ALOE

While most people know of *Aloe vera* (see p141), which among other things is used in sunburn remedies and skin creams, this popular species is just one of many varieties of aloe available to house plant collectors. Most species produce a decorative rosette of large, thick, fleshy leaves, which can be bright green, variegated, or mottled. Plants may be stemless, with the leafy rosette growing at ground level, or taller with branched stems. Clusters of tubular flowers, which are usually yellow, orange, pink, or red, are held on tall stems in spring or summer, although on some species the blooms may not develop when plants are grown indoors.

TEMPERATURE 5–30°C (41–86°F).

LIGHT Position in full sun, but provide some shade in summer.

WATERING From spring to early autumn, water when the surface of compost is dry. Reduce watering in autumn and winter so that the compost is just moist and the leaves do not shrivel.

FEEDING Apply a half-strength cactus fertilizer every month from spring to late summer.

COMPOST Plant in cactus compost, or a 50:50 mix of loam-based (John Innes No .2) compost and 4mm grit.

FLOWERING Plants are more likely to flower when given cool conditions in winter at a temperature of 5–10°C (41–50°F).

PROPAGATION Take offsets or leaf cuttings.

COMMON PROBLEMS Plants are prone to rot if grown in wet compost. Check regularly for mealy bugs and scale insects.

ALOE ARISTATA AGM
syn. *Aloe ellenbergeri;*
Aloe longiaristata
Lace aloe

The lace aloe takes its name from the white spots on its dainty green foliage. These form a horizontal striped pattern that sets the plant apart from it plain-leaved cousins. Its tubular orange-red flowers, which form on long stems in autumn, also appear more reliably than in some other species.

HEIGHT AND SPREAD Up to 20 x 20cm (8 x 8in).

CARE NOTES See left.

ALOE ARISTATA 'GREEN PEARL'
syn. *Aloe* 'Cosmo'
Lace aloe

Sold under the names 'Green Pearl' or 'Cosmo', this pretty lace aloe cultivar has elegant dark green leaves, with dainty white spots dotted along the edges and horizontal bands covering the outer surfaces. Like the species, *Aloe aristata* (see left), it also produces tubular, orange-red flowers in autumn.

HEIGHT AND SPREAD Up to 20 x 20cm (8 x 8in).

CARE NOTES See left.

ALOE ERINACEA
syn. *Aloe melanacantha* var. *erinacea*

Look out for this spiky little plant, which produces ball-shaped rosettes of brownish-green triangular leaves edged with sharp spines. The leaves curve inwards and mature plants may form small clusters of rosettes. Plants grown indoors are reluctant to bloom; those that do will bear bright red summer flowers, which turn yellow after opening.

HEIGHT AND SPREAD Up to 25 x 25cm (10 x 10in).

CARE NOTES See opposite.

CAUTION Wear cactus gloves to handle this plant.

ALOE HUMILIS
syn. *Aloe perfoliata* var. *humilis*
Spider aloe

The spider aloe is a small, compact plant that makes a great companion for other dwarf succulents and cacti. Its pale blue-green leaves grow vertically but curve slightly inwards. They feature grey-green raised bumps and are edged with thin, soft, white spines. In spring, clusters of drooping, tubular, bright orange-red flowers appear on tall stems.

HEIGHT AND SPREAD Up to 20 x 20cm (8 x 8in).

CARE NOTES See opposite.

ALOE PLICATILIS AGM
Fan aloe

This unusual species grows as a shrub or small tree in its native South Africa, and even as a potted house plant can grow to 1.5m (5ft) tall. It produces a woody trunk and spineless, strap-shaped, pale green to blue-grey leaves arranged in a fan shape, hence its common name. Tubular, bright red flowers that fade to yellow-green form on tall stems that rise up from the leafy fans in spring.

HEIGHT AND SPREAD Up to 1.5 x 0.9m (5 x 3ft).

CARE NOTES See p138.

ALOE VARIEGATA AGM
syn. *Aloe variegata* var. *haworthii*
Partridge breast aloe; Tiger aloe

The striped white and dark green bands on outward-curving leaves give the partridge breast aloe a distinctive look, while its lack of spines or sharp-toothed edges make it a goodcandidate for homes with children or pets. The orange-red flowers appear reliably in spring or summer on tall stems.

HEIGHT AND SPREAD Up to 20 x 20cm (8 x 8in).

CARE NOTES See p138.

ALOE VERA AGM

syn. *Aloe perfoliata* var. *vera*
Barbados aloe

While the rosettes of fleshy dull green leaves with soft spiny margins may not look as exciting as some others in this group, the Barbados aloe is an easy and useful plant to grow at home. The fleshy centres of the leaves can be used to treat mild burns, including sunburn, and any foliage removed for such a purpose will soon be replaced by new growth. The plant's tubular greenish-yellow flowers rarely appear on plants grown indoors.

HEIGHT AND SPREAD Up to 60 x 60cm (24 x 24in).

CARE NOTES See p138.

APTENIA

Native to South Africa, these small shrubby succulents develop trailing or climbing stems covered with tiny heart-shaped leaves. Unlike many succulents, this pretty trailer is grown for its prolific summer flowers as much as for its foliage. The small daisy-like blooms develop at the tips of the leafy stems and come in many colours, including pink, purple, yellow, or white.

TEMPERATURE -7°C–30°C (19–86°F); plants can tolerate a few degrees of frost if the soil is dry.

LIGHT Position in full sun or filtered sun; provide some shade in summer.

WATERING From spring to early autumn, water when the top of compost is dry. Reduce watering in autumn and winter so that the compost is just moist and the leaves do not shrivel.

FEEDING Apply a general-purpose granular fertilizer in spring at half the dose recommended on the label.

COMPOST Plant in cactus compost, or a 50:50 mix of loam-based (John Innes No. 2) compost and 4mm grit.

FLOWERING Flowers appear freely without any special treatment.

PROPAGATION Take stem cuttings.

COMMON PROBLEMS These plants will rot if left in wet compost. Pests to look out for include mealybugs and spider mites.

APTENIA CORDIFOLIA 'VARIEGATA'

syn. *Mesembryanthemum cordifolium* 'Variegata'
Baby sun rose

The beautiful flowing stems of white-edged, heart-shaped leaves and bright pink spring and summer flowers create a year-round feature when this plant it grown in a tall pot or hanging basket. If including this plant in a mixed succulent display, plant it in a separate pot; it is very vigorous and may swamp its neighbours if grouped with other plants in a single container.

HEIGHT AND SPREAD Up to 10 x 90cm (4 x 36in).

CARE NOTES See left.

CEROPEGIA

Most *Ceropegia* are grown for their trailing, wiry stems (a few species are upright) and patterned, heart-shaped, fleshy leaves, which make beautiful hanging basket displays. Very easy to grow, these succulents also produce curious tubular flowers that look like old-fashioned tobacco pipes and develop along the length of the stems in summer.

TEMPERATURE 8–30°C (46–86°F)

LIGHT Position in full sun, but provide some shade in summer.

WATERING During the spring and summer, water when the top 1cm (½in) of compost is dry. In autumn and winter, keep the compost just moist enough to ensure the leaves do not shrivel.

FEEDING Apply a half-strength all-purpose liquid fertilizer once a month from late spring to late summer.

COMPOST Plant in cactus compost, or a 50:50 mix of loam-based (John Innes No. 2) compost and 4mm grit.

FLOWERING Flowers appear freely if plants are watered adequately and given a little fertilizer.

PROPAGATION Sow seed or take stem cuttings.

COMMON PROBLEMS These plants will rot if left in wet compost. Pests to look out for include mealybugs and spider mite.

CEROPEGIA LINEARIS subsp. WOODII AGM

syn. *Ceropegia woodii*
String of hearts

As the name suggests, string of hearts produces long slender stems covered with heart-shaped leaves. These are green and decorated with cream-coloured lacy patterns on the upper surface, and purple underneath, creating a beautiful two-tone effect. The pink and purple tubular flowers appear in summer. Very easy to grow, this plant tolerates neglect and will endure long periods of drought. Place it on a high shelf or in a hanging basket where its long stems can flow freely without becoming too tangled.

HEIGHT AND SPREAD Up to 5cm x 2m (2in x 6ft 6in).

CARE NOTES See left.

COTYLEDON

With their softly textured leaves and colourful flowers, this group of small- to medium-sized African succulents are popular house plants. The foliage of some *Cotyledon* species is covered with a powdery bloom or downy hairs, giving the plants a velvety appearance, while the tubular flowers of these decorative plants are typically orange or pink and usually appear in summer.

TEMPERATURE 5–30°C (41–86°F); will tolerate -2°C (28°F) for short periods if soil is dry.

LIGHT Position in full sun but provide some shade in summer.

WATERING Water from below from late spring to autumn when the top 1cm (½in) of compost feels dry. In winter reduce watering so that the compost is almost dry.

FEEDING Apply a half-strength balanced liquid fertilizer once a month from late spring to late summer.

COMPOST Plant in cactus compost, or a 50:50 mix of loam-based (John Innes No. 2) compost and 4mm grit.

FLOWERING Plants will flower without any special treatment.

PROPAGATION Sow seed or take stem or leaf cuttings.

COMMON PROBLEMS Plants are susceptible to root rot if overwatered or left sitting in wet compost. Check plants regularly for mealybugs.

COTYLEDON ORBICULATA
syn. *Cotyledon ramosa*
Pig's ear; Dog's ear

The pig's ear gets its name from its grey-green oval leaves, which are covered with a white waxy coating and edged with a line of red. A tall, branched shrub, this *Cotyledon* may reach over 1m (3ft) in height, but its size can be restricted by growing it in a pot. Small bell-shaped orange-red flowers, which are also covered with a waxy bloom, appear on long stems in late summer and autumn.

HEIGHT AND SPREAD Up to 1m x 60cm (3 x 2ft).

CARE NOTES See left.

CAUTION This plant is poisonous if consumed.

COTYLEDON UNDULATA
syn. *Cotyledon orbiculata* f. *undulata*
Silver ruffles; Silver crown

Silver ruffles has beautiful fan-shaped grey leaves with crimped edges and a soft silver–white powdery coating, hence its common name. Its orange or yellow flowers appear in summer.

HEIGHT AND SPREAD Up to 50 x 40cm (20 x 16in).

CARE NOTES See left.

CAUTION This plant is poisonous if consumed.

CRASSULA

Many *Crassula* plants are tall branched shrubs with colourful foliage, while others form dense rosettes, and some dwarf varieties take on a geometric shape. The foliage varies depending on the species, and can be round, oval, spear- or heart-shaped. *Crassula* also produces showy clusters of star-like white to pink flowers in spring to summer, although plants grown indoors may be reluctant to bloom. If the brittle stems are broken off, they will make good cuttings and are easy to propagate (see p203).

TEMPERATURE 5–30°C (41–86°F); keep cool but frost-free in winter, although plants will tolerate -2°C (28°F) for short periods if soil is dry.

LIGHT Position in full sun. Provide some shade in summer.

WATERING Water from late spring to autumn only when the top 2cm (¾in) of compost is dry; reduce watering in winter so that the compost is almost dry but the leaves are not shrivelled.

FEEDING Apply a general-purpose granular fertilizer at half the recommended dose in late spring.

COMPOST Plant in cactus compost, or a 50:50 mix of loam-based (John Innes No. 2) compost and 4mm grit.

FLOWERING House plants rarely flower.

PROPAGATION Take stem or leaf cuttings.

COMMON PROBLEMS Plants are prone to rot if overwatered or left sitting in wet compost. Check them regularly for mealybugs.

CRASSULA ARBORESCENS
syn. *Cotyledon arborescens*
Silver jade plant

The silver jade plant is a branched, tree-shaped shrub with thick, round, shimmering silver-grey leaves. The foliage may also be edged with a maroon strip and feature reddish spots on the upper surfaces. Clusters of starry pinkish-white flowers may appear in spring on mature plants grown outside in warm climates. Look out for the popular subspecies, *Crassula arborescens* subsp. *undulatifolia* (pictured below), which has more elliptical-shaped leaves with twisted edges.

HEIGHT AND SPREAD Up to 1 x 0.6m (40 x 24in).

CARE NOTES See left.

CRASSULA OVATA AGM

syn. *Cotyledon ovata*
Friendship tree; Jade plant;
Money plant

The friendship tree has a quiet charm with its branched stems covered with thick dark green oval leaves, often edged in red. Flat clusters of small, starry white or light pink flowers may develop in late summer on mature plants grown outside.

HEIGHT AND SPREAD Up to 1.5 x 0.9m (5 x 3ft).

CARE NOTES See opposite.

CRASSULA OVATA 'HOBBIT'

Jade plant 'Hobbit'

'Hobbit' has the same tree-like habit as its parent, the friendship tree (see left), but it sports curious tube-like leaves. Not quite as large as its parent, it is a better candidate for smaller spaces.

HEIGHT AND SPREAD Up to 90 x 80cm (36 x 32in).

CARE NOTES See opposite.

CRASSULA OVATA 'HUMMEL'S SUNSET' AGM
syn. *Crassula ovata* 'Sunset'
Jade plant 'Hummel's Sunset'

A popular cultivar of *Crassula ovata*, 'Hummel's Sunset' has bright yellow-edged green leaves suffused with red that create an eye-catching tricoloured effect. It bears small starry white or pale pink flowers but these are rarely produced on plants grown indoors.

HEIGHT AND SPREAD Up to 90 x 80cm (36 x 32in).

CARE NOTES See p144; leaf colours will fade if kept in poor light.

CRASSULA PELLUCIDA subsp. MARGINALIS f. RUBRA
syn. *Crassula marginalis rubra* 'Variegata'

Look out for this *Crassula* if you need a colourful succulent with long, cascading stems for a hanging basket or tall pot. Tiny red-edged, heart-shaped leaves, which are purplish-pink with a dash of yellow or green, cover the stems to provide year-round interest. White flowers may emerge from the stem tips in summer.

HEIGHT AND SPREAD Up to 15 x 45cm (6 x 18in).

CARE NOTES See p144.

CRASSULA PERFORATA AGM
syn. *Crassula perfossa;*
Crassula nealeana
String of buttons; Necklace plant

Originally from South Africa, the stems
of the string of buttons initially grow
upright and then sprawl to form a loose
fountain shape. Its small oval leaves are
grey-green with pink edges, and look a
little like buttons threaded on the stem,
hence its common name. Tiny star-shaped
white flowers appear in spring.

HEIGHT AND SPREAD: Up to 45 x 45cm
(18 x 18in).

CARE NOTES See p144.

CRASSULA PERFOLIATA var. FALCATA AGM
syn. *Crassula falcata* 'Rochea';
Crassula perfoliata var. *minor*
Propeller plant; Airplane plant

The unusual arrangement of sickle-
shaped, silvery grey–green leaves gives
the propeller plant its common name,
and its quirky appearance can create
quite a talking point. As the plant
matures, the foliage grows in more
horizontal layers, but still looks amazing.
Clusters of small fragrant scarlet flowers
may appear in late summer on plants
grown outside.

HEIGHT AND SPREAD Up to 90 x 90cm
(3 x 3ft).

CARE NOTES See p144.

CRASSULA RUPESTRIS subsp. MARNIERIANA
syn. *Crassula marnieriana*
Jade necklace plant

A good choice for small spaces or a
hanging basket, the gently trailing stems
of the jade necklace plant are composed
of square bead-like green leaves, often
suffused with red. Quite the show-stopper
despite its diminutive size, it is very
easy to care for and a good choice for
beginners. Small star-shaped pink flowers
may appear in the summer.

HEIGHT AND SPREAD Up to 10 x 20cm
(4 x 8in).

CARE NOTES See p144.

CURIO

Trailing or upright, the most commonly grown *Curio* species have intriguing leaves that look either like peas or beads, or fat little fingers. The foliage may be blue-green, grey-green, or bright green, and all species will add texture and colour to a succulent and cacti collection. Plants often become leggy with age, but can be trimmed back annually to keep them bushy.

TEMPERATURE 5–30°C (41–86°F); plants will tolerate -2°C (28°F) for short periods if soil is dry.

LIGHT Position in full sun or light shade; place in light shade in summer.

WATERING During the spring and summer, water when the top 1cm (½in) of compost is dry. In autumn and winter keep the compost almost dry, watering just enough to prevent the leaves shrivelling.

FEEDING Apply a half-strength liquid fertilizer once a year in late spring.

COMPOST Plant in cactus compost, or a 50:50 mix of loam-based (John Innes No. 2) compost and 4mm grit.

FLOWERING Flowers rarely appear on house plants.

PROPAGATION Take offsets or stem cuttings.

COMMON PROBLEMS These plants will rot in wet compost, and the leaves can become swollen if given too much water. Check plants regularly for mealybugs.

CURIO REPENS

syn. *Senecio serpens*;
Senecio talinoides subsp. *mandraliscae*
Blue chalk sticks

Often labelled under their synonym *Senecio serpens*, blue chalk sticks are accurately named, as the white coating on their blue-green cylindrical leaves looks like chalk dust. The leafy stems form large clusters and can quickly fill a wide pot. Small white flowers may appear in summer.

HEIGHT AND SPREAD Up to 20 x 30cm (8 x 12in).

CARE NOTES See left.

CAUTION The leaves are poisonous to humans and pets if consumed.

DUDLEYA

Often mistaken for *Echeveria* (see pp150-54), *Dudleya* thrive on neglect and are extremely easy to care for. They are grown for their colourful leafy rosettes, which are often in tones of green or blue-grey. Some plants are branching, producing groups of rosettes on low-growing stems, while others form solitary rosettes. The spring flowers are usually yellow, enclosed by pinkish-red bracts (petal-like modified leaves), and held on long colourful stems. *Dudleya* grow on rocky outcrops and cliffs in hot, dry southwestern US states and Mexico, and will become dormant in high summer temperatures.

TEMPERATURE 5-30°C (41-86°F)

LIGHT Position in full sun; place in light shade in summer.

WATERING From spring to autumn, water when the top 1cm (½in) of compost is dry. In winter keep the compost almost dry, watering just enough to prevent the leaves shrivelling.

FEEDING Apply a half-strength liquid fertilizer once a month from late winter to late spring.

COMPOST Plant in cactus compost, or a 50:50 mix of loam-based (John Innes No. 2) compost and 4mm grit.

FLOWERING Flowers will form without any special treatment.

PROPAGATION Sow seed or take offsets.

COMMON PROBLEMS These plants will rot in wet compost. Pests to look out for include mealybugs and aphids.

CURIO ROWLEYANUS

syn. *Senecio rowleyanus*
String of beads; String of pearls

The string of beads is one of a kind. Its eye-catching fountain of green pearl-shaped leaves on wiry, cascading stems will flow gracefully over the sides of a tall container or basket. This easy-care plant is ideal for beginners; the stems are quite brittle but this *Curio* will soldier on regardless if they break off. The only problem is keeping the plant in check – its stems can trail for over 1m (4ft), so hang it up high or place it on a stand.

HEIGHT AND SPREAD Up to 10 x 90cm (4 x 36in).

CARE NOTES See opposite.

CAUTION The leaves are poisonous to humans and pets if consumed.

DUDLEYA BRITTONII AGM

Giant chalk dudleya;
Silver dollar plant

Grow the colourful giant chalk dudleya for its beautiful sea-green leaves, which are covered with a white powdery coating that resembles chalk, hence the name. The coating reflects the sun, helping the plant to withstand heat and drought. Avoid touching the leaves, however, as fingers marks can cause permanent blemishes. In spring, long red spikes of starry yellow or orange flowers, cupped in pink bracts (petal-like modified leaves), rise up from the leafy rosettes. As the plants mature, the old dead leaves hang on to the main stem and can be carefully removed.

HEIGHT AND SPREAD Up to 45 x 45cm (18 x 18in).

CARE NOTES See left.

ECHEVERIA

Loved for their beautiful leaf rosettes, which in some species look like water-lily flowers, *Echeveria* include many easy-care varieties in a spectrum of foliage colours and textures. The rosettes quickly multiply to form small clusters, and the lantern-shaped flowers reliably appear each spring or summer without any special treatment. Ideal for beginners, a range of contrasting *Echeveria* species can be used to create a trouble-free windowsill collection.

TEMPERATURE 5–30°C (41–86°F); some species tolerate short periods below freezing at -3°C (27°F) if the soil is dry.

LIGHT Position in full sun; place in light shade in summer.

WATERING During the spring and summer, water when the top 1cm (½in) of compost is dry. In autumn and winter keep the compost almost dry, watering just enough to prevent the leaves from shrivelling.

FEEDING Apply a half-strength liquid fertilizer once a month from late spring to late summer.

COMPOST Plant in cactus compost, or a 50:50 mix of loam-based (John Innes No. 2) compost and 4mm grit.

FLOWERING Flowers will form without any special treatment.

PROPAGATION Sow seed or take offsets.

COMMON PROBLEMS These plants will rot in wet compost. Check plants regularly for mealybugs.

ECHEVERIA AGAVOIDES AGM
Moulded wax

The curious name of the moulded wax plant refers to the waxy coating that covers its rosettes of thick red-tipped pale green leaves. Also look out for the more colourful cultivar *Echeveria agavoides* 'Red Edge', the leaves of which are outlined in red. Both produce dainty red summer flowers with yellow tips.

HEIGHT AND SPREAD Up to 12 x 30cm (5 x 12in).

CARE NOTES See left.

ECHEVERIA AGAVOIDES 'RED TAURUS'
Moulded wax 'Red Taurus'

'Red Taurus' (sometimes sold as just 'Taurus') has dark red to reddish-green leaves and bears red flowers in summer.

HEIGHT AND SPREAD Up to 12 x 30cm (5 x 12in).

CARE NOTES See opposite.

ECHEVERIA AGAVOIDES 'EBONY'
Moulded wax 'Ebony'

The smouldering good looks of this cultivar are created by an eye-catching colour combination of pale green foliage with dark red tips. The yellow-edged red flowers appear in summer.

HEIGHT AND SPREAD Up to 10 x 15cm (4 x 6in).

CARE NOTES See opposite.

ECHEVERIA AMOENA
syn. *Echeveria purpusii*; *Echeveria pusilla*
Hen and chicks

The tiny rosettes of this pretty little *Echeveria* are made up of fat, diamond-shaped blue–green leaves, which may be tinged with pink if the plant is grown in a little shade. In late spring, pale yellow and coral flowers produce a dazzling effect when they appear on the end of bright red stems. The long-lasting blooms are open for about a month.

HEIGHT AND SPREAD Up to 2.5 x 5cm (1 x 2in).

CARE NOTES See opposite.

ECHEVERIA 'BLACK KNIGHT'
Hen and chicks
'Black Knight'

A rare but much sought-after *Echeveria*, this little succulent produces rosettes of dark chocolate-brown outer leaves with bright green nearer the centre. The dark red flowers add to the rich colour combination in summer.

HEIGHT AND SPREAD Up to 10 x 20cm (4 x 8in).

CARE NOTES See p150.

ECHEVERIA COLORATA AGM
syn. *Echeveria colorata* f. *colorata*;
Echeveria lindsayana
Hen and chicks

The rosettes of this award-winning echeveria are relatively large, and produce silvery blue-green leaves tipped with pinky red hues. The leaves arch slightly upwards, causing the rosettes to look a little like flower heads. Long-stemmed pink blooms appear in early summer.

HEIGHT AND SPREAD Up to 30 x 40cm (12 x 16in).

CARE NOTES See p150.

ECHEVERIA ELEGANS AGM
Mexican snowball;
Mexican gem

The rosettes of the Mexican snowball are made up of silvery, ice-blue, spoon-shaped leaves that glisten in the sun. Pink flowers, tipped with yellow, appear in early spring on long pink stems, creating a colourful display.

HEIGHT AND SPREAD Up to 10 x 20cm (4 x 8in).

CARE NOTES See p150.

ECHEVERIA LAUI AGM
Hen and chicks

One of the most beautiful species, *Echeveria laui* features chubby, spoon-shaped leaves in a sophisticated shade of pale blue. Although the leaves look soft, try not to touch them, as fingers can leave permanent unsightly marks on the waxy coating. Pink and orange summer flowers make a striking contrast to the pastel foliage colour.

HEIGHT AND SPREAD Up to 10 x 15cm (4 x 6in).

CARE NOTES See p150.

ECHEVERIA LEUCOTRICHA AGM
Chenille plant; White-plush plant

The soft, downy foliage of the chenille plant gives it a velvety appearance, inviting you to stroke it. The tactile texture is produced by silvery hairs that cover the rosettes, turning brown at the tips of the leaves. These provide a foil for the orange-red flowers when they appear in summer.

HEIGHT AND SPREAD Up to 15 x 30cm (6 x 12in).

CARE NOTES See p150.

ECHEVERIA LILACINA AGM
Ghost echeveria

Prized for its unusual colour, the ghost echeveria stands out from its cousins with its neat rosettes of spoon-shaped leaves in a pearlescent shade of blue, which becomes infused with lilac or purple when the plant is grown in full sun. Showy pinkish-orange spring blooms appear in spring.

HEIGHT AND SPREAD Up to 12 x 20cm (4 x 10in).

CARE NOTES See p150.

ECHEVERIA. SECUNDA var. GLAUCA 'COMPTON CAROUSEL' AGM

Glaucous echeveria
'Compton Carousel'

'Compton Carousel' makes a striking impression with its cream and blue-green patterned rosettes. The margins of older leaves become tinged with pink, adding to the colourful mix. In almost all other respects it is the same as its parent plant (see left), although it is a little smaller in stature.

HEIGHT AND SPREAD Up to 15 x 30cm (6 x 12in).

CARE NOTES See p150.

ECHEVERIA SECUNDA var. GLAUCA

syn. *Echeveria glauca*
Glaucous echeveria

Highly popular and widely available, the glaucous echeveria is aptly named, as it forms clusters of pale blue-grey leaf rosettes. Larger than many members of the *Echeveria* family, it makes an attractive house plant in a wide pot. The red and yellow flowers appear in summer on pinkish-purple stems.

HEIGHT AND SPREAD Up to 30 x 45cm (12 x 18in).

CARE NOTES See p150.

ECHEVERIA SETOSA AGM

Mexican firecracker

The hairy texture of the Mexican firecracker give the tiny leaves a frosted look. This *Echeveria* also produces vibrant red flowers with bright yellow tips in summer, hence its common name.

HEIGHT AND SPREAD Up to 5 x 30cm (2 x 12in).

CARE NOTES See p150.

EUPHORBIA

A huge and varied group of plants, *Euphorbia* range from desert-dwelling cactus look-alikes to leafy hardy perennials and towering tree-like species. The succulents grown as house plants generally fall into the group that resemble cacti, which evolved in African deserts to cope with the same hot, dry conditions as their prickly American relatives. *Euphorbia* are generally grown for their foliage more than their flowers, which are often small and not very showy, although some have colourful bracts (petal-like leaves). All *Euphorbia* have poisonous, milky, latex-like sap, which irritates the eyes and skin on contact and is toxic if consumed.

TEMPERATURE 5–30°C (23–86°F) for tender species; some *Euphorbia* grown as house plants must be kept at 10°C (50°F) or higher.

LIGHT Position in full sun; place in light shade in summer.

WATERING During the spring and summer, water when the top 2cm (¾in) of compost is dry. In autumn and winter keep the compost almost dry.

FEEDING Apply a half-strength cactus fertilizer once a month during late spring and summer.

COMPOST Plant in cactus compost, or a 50:50 mix of loam-based (John Innes No. 2) compost and 4mm grit.

FLOWERING Flowers will appear on house plants without any special treatment.

PROPAGATION Sow seed or take stem cuttings.

COMMON PROBLEMS These plants will rot in wet compost. Pests to look out for include scale insects and mealybugs.

EUPHORBIA BUPLEURIFOLIA
syn. *Euphorbia proteifolia*, *Tithymalus bupleurifolius*
Pine cone plant

The long green leaves of this sculptural plant sprout from what look like pine cones or pineapples, hence the name. The "pine cone" is, in fact, a modified stem (caudex) designed to store water. Attractive yellow–green flowers, held in green bracts on slim stems, appear in spring. This plant is deciduous so don't worry if the leaves fall off in winter, as they will reappear the following spring.

HEIGHT AND SPREAD Up to 30 x 30cm (12 x 12in).

CARE NOTES See left; do not allow temperature to fall below 10°C (50°F) and apply full strength doses of fertilizer rather than half strength.

CAUTION Wear cactus gloves when handling this plant. The milky sap a skin and eye irritant, and toxic if consumed.

EUPHORBIA ENOPLA
Pincushion euphorbia

The sharp bright red spines of this cactus are more like swords than pins, and it makes a dramatic statement in a mixed collection. Mature plants develop into large branched shrubs with thick grey-green column-shaped ribbed stems, although they will remain smaller if grown in a pot. Position this euphorbia where it will have space to grow without causing injury.

HEIGHT AND SPREAD Up to 90 x 60cm (3 x 2ft).

CARE NOTES See left; grow in light shade for the brightest spines.

CAUTION Wear cactus gloves when handling this plant. The sap is a skin and eye irritant, and toxic if consumed.

EUPHORBIA HORRIDA AGM
African milk barrel

The blue-green ribbed stems of the aptly named *Euphorbia horrida* are covered with vicious long reddish-brown spines and contain a poisonous milky sap. Its spiny armour, beautiful colouring and small yellow and green summer flowers combine to create an eye-catching focal point.

HEIGHT AND SPREAD Up to 75 x 90cm (30 x 36in).

CARE NOTES See p155.

CAUTION Wear cactus gloves when handling this plant. The milky sap is a skin and eye irritant, and toxic if consumed.

EUPHORBIA OBESA AGM
Basketball; Golf ball

This little beauty produces clusters of ball-shaped blue- or brown-green stems with plaid-like patterning. As the basketball grows, it becomes more cone-shaped, but produces offsets alongside the parent plant, creating fascinating clusters. Tiny flowers appear at the top of the plant, which eventually form fig-shaped seedheads, adding another unusual feature to this unique little plant.

HEIGHT AND SPREAD Up to 20 x 10cm (8 x 4in).

CARE NOTES See p155.

CAUTION Wear cactus gloves when handling this plant. The milky sap is a skin and eye irritant, and toxic if consumed.

EUPHORBIA TRIGONA
syn. *Euphorbia hermentiana*
African milk tree

The tall dark green branched stems of the African milk tree feature three or four prominent ribs, from which sprout sharp spines and small spoon-shaped leaves in spring and summer. This plant is deciduous, which means that the foliage will drop in autumn and reappear the following spring. When grown as a house plant, it will not produce flowers.

HEIGHT AND SPREAD Up to 2 x 1m (6ft 6in x 3ft 4in).

CARE NOTES See p155.

CAUTION Wear cactus gloves when handling this plant. The milky sap is a skin and eye irritant, and toxic if consumed.

EUPHORBIA TIRUCALLI
syn. *Arthrothamnus tirucalli; Tirucalia tirucalli*
Pencil cactus; Pencil tree

A tree-sized succulent in its native Africa, as a potted house plant the pencil cactus will grow to just 1m (3ft) or so in height. The tangled mass of smooth, pencil-thick, cylindrical stems produce its curious, spindly silhouette. In young plants, the stems are also covered with tiny leaves but these fall off as the plant matures. The yellowish flowers rarely appear on plants grown indoors.

HEIGHT AND SPREAD Up to 90 x 75cm (36 x 30in).

CARE NOTES See p155.

CAUTION Wear cactus gloves when handling this plant. The milky sap is a skin and eye irritant, and toxic if consumed.

FAUCARIA

These unusual succulents produce clumps of rosettes made up of tooth-edged green leaves that are arranged to resemble an open jaw. Its daisy-like flowers, which are usually yellow, bloom for many weeks. *Faucaria* need more water than many succulents during their growth period in spring and summer, but apart from that, they are easy to care for and an ideal choice for beginners.

TEMPERATURE 5–30°C (41–86°F); they can tolerate freezing conditions of -5°C (23°F) if the soil is dry.

LIGHT Position in full sun from autumn to spring; provide light shade in summer.

WATERING During spring and summer, water when the top of the compost feels dry. In autumn and winter keep the compost almost dry, watering just enough to prevent the leaves shrivelling.

FEEDING Apply a half-strength liquid fertilizer once a year in spring.

COMPOST Plant in cactus compost, or a 50:50 mix of loam-based (John Innes No. 2) compost and 4mm grit.

FLOWERING Flowers appear annually if plants are watered and fertilized correctly (see above).

PROPAGATION Sow seed or take offsets.

COMMON PROBLEMS These plants will rot in wet compost. Pests to look out for include mealybugs.

FAUCARIA TUBERCULOSA AGM

syn. *Faucaria felina* subsp. *tuberculosa*, *Mesembryanthemum tuberculosum*
Warty tiger's jaws

Similar in many respects to *Faucaria tigrina* AGM (see left), the leaves of the warty tiger's jaws are covered with white tubercules (raised bumps), giving this plant the warty appearance for which it is named. It produces yellow flowers that appear in autumn and open only on sunny afternoons.

HEIGHT AND SPREAD Up to 15 x 20cm (6 x 8in).

CARE NOTES See above left.

FAUCARIA TIGRINA AGM

syn. *Mesembryanthemum tigrinum*
Tiger's jaws

A great gift for children, the little leaves of the tiger's jaws look like open mouths lined with sharp curved teeth, although these spines are actually soft and harmless. The triangular leaves are light green with white flecks, although they may turn purple if grown in strong sun. In autumn, silky daisy-like yellow flowers bloom over many weeks, opening each day in the afternoon when it is sunny and closing in the evening.

HEIGHT AND SPREAD Up to 15 x 20cm (6 x 8in).

CARE NOTES See above.

FENESTRARIA

A native of Namibia, this plant group contains just one species, *Fenestraria rhopalophylla*. It takes its Latin name from the transparent window-like area at the tip of each stemless leaf. In the wild, these leaves are buried beneath the sand to protect them from the heat, while their windows peek out above the surface to photosynthesize and feed the plant. When kept as a house plant, the whole leaf will grow above the soil surface. Golden-yellow flowers appear in winter. Often mistaken for *Lithops* (see pp170–71), *Fenestraria* is just as easy to grow.

TEMPERATURE 5–30°C (41–86°F); can tolerate -4°C (25°F) for short periods if the soil is dry.

LIGHT Position in full sun. Provide light shade in summer.

WATERING During the spring and autumn, water when the top 2cm (¾in) of compost is dry. In summer and winter, keep the compost almost dry, watering just enough to prevent the leaves shrivelling. Ensure plants have good air circulation.

FEEDING Apply a half-strength liquid fertilizer once a year in spring.

COMPOST Plant in cactus compost, or a 50:50 mix of loam-based (John Innes No. 2) compost and 4mm grit.

FLOWERING Flowers appear annually without any special treatment.

PROPAGATION Sow seed or take offsets.

COMMON PROBLEMS These plants will rot in wet compost. Watch out for mealybugs.

FENESTRARIA RHOPALOPHYLLA subsp. AURANTIACA AGM
Baby's toes

The stemless pale green leaves of this plant each have the characteristic transparent window at the top. Growing in a pot, these leaves form small colonies that are said to resemble baby's toes, hence the name. The relatively large golden yellow daisy-like flowers appear on short, slim stems from winter to early spring.

HEIGHT AND SPREAD Up to 5 x 15cm (2 x 6in).

CARE NOTES See left.

x GASTERHAWORTHIA

A beautiful hybrid succulent and very easy to grow, x *Gasterhaworthia* is a cross between *Gasteria* (see opposite) and *Haworthia* (see p163). It produces rosettes of fat, triangular leaves, often decorated with spots or subtle patterns. It also produces clusters of tubular flowers on long stems in spring or summer, but these are rarely seen on house plants.

TEMPERATURE 5–27°C (41–80°F); can tolerate freezing conditions of -1°C (30°F) for a short while if the soil is dry.

LIGHT Position in a bright spot, out of direct sunlight.

WATERING During the spring and summer, water when the top 2cm (¾in) of compost is dry. In autumn and winter, keep the compost almost dry, watering just enough to prevent the leaves shrivelling.

FEEDING Apply a half-strength liquid fertilizer once a year in late spring.

COMPOST Plant in cactus compost, or a 50:50 mix of loam-based (John Innes No. 2) compost and 4mm grit.

FLOWERING Flowers rarely appear on house plants.

PROPAGATION Take offsets or leaf cuttings.

COMMON PROBLEMS These plants will rot in wet compost. Look out for mealybugs.

x GASTERHAWORTHIA 'ROYAL HIGHNESS'
syn. x *Gasteraloe* 'Royal Highness'

'Royal Highness' features fat triangular dark green leaves that turn a reddish hue in bright sunlight, but it is the white tubercles (round raised bumps) that have made this cultivar so popular. These spots form a horizontal striped pattern, creating a striking combination of texture and colour.

HEIGHT AND SPREAD Up to 15 x 15cm (6 x 6in).

CARE NOTES See left.

GASTERIA

Compact and easy to grow, *Gasteria* species have thick strap- or tongue-shaped leaves, arranged in round or linear rosettes, which often feature tubercles (raised bumps) or speckles. Plants produce flowers that are generally pink or red and look like little stomachs with a tube at the end, hence the plant's name (which means "stomach" in Latin). Despite the grisly association, the blooms are quite pretty, and appear in clusters on long stems in spring.

TEMPERATURE 5–27°C (41–80°F); can tolerate freezing conditions of -1°C (30°F) for a short while if the soil is dry.

LIGHT Position in a bright spot out of direct sunlight.

WATERING During the spring and summer, water when the top 2cm (¾in) of compost is dry. In autumn and winter, keep the compost almost dry, watering just enough to prevent the leaves shrivelling. Ensure the plants have good air circulation.

FEEDING Apply a half-strength liquid fertilizer once a year in late spring.

COMPOST Plant in cactus compost, or a 50:50 mix of loam-based (John Innes No. 2) compost and 4mm grit.

FLOWERING Flowers will appear on mature plants, given sufficient water and a small amount of fertilizer.

PROPAGATION Take offsets or leaf cuttings.

COMMON PROBLEMS Look out for mealybugs.

GASTERIA BICOLOR
syn. *Aloe bicolor; Aloe bowieana; Aloe dictyodes; Aloe lingua*

The strappy leaves of this plant are green with white mottled stripes, producing a decorative bicoloured effect. The foliage may turn red if the plant is placed in too much light. Tall stems of reddish-pink and green flowers appear on mature plants in spring.

HEIGHT AND SPREAD Up to 40 x 50cm (16 x 20in).

CARE NOTES See left.

GASTERIA BRACHYPHYLLA
syn. *Aloe brachyphylla*
Ox-tongue

The ox-tongue is a compact species with the blunt strap-shaped leaves arranged in a linear formation that is typical of many *Gasteria*. The smooth, shiny, dark green foliage features pale cream speckles that form a horizontal striped pattern. Pink flowers appear in spring.

HEIGHT AND SPREAD Up to 20 x 20cm (8 x 8in).

CARE NOTES See left.

GASTERIA 'LITTLE WARTY' AGM

syn. *Gasteria batesiana* 'Little Warty'
Ox-tongue 'Little Warty'

'Little Warty' has tongue-shaped leaves with pointed ends. The foliage is dark green with pale olive-green edges and raised white speckles or streaks. The pink and green flowers appear in spring on mature plants.

HEIGHT AND SPREAD Up to 20 x 20cm (8 x 8in).

CARE NOTES See p161.

GRAPTOPETALUM

Elegant and colourful, the leafy rosettes of *Graptopetalum* look a little like water lily flowers, although a few have round, pebble-shaped foliage. Their beautiful colours range from pale lilac-grey and silver to lime and blue-green – some also feature variegated foliage. Unlike most succulents, *Graptopetalum* are best grown out of direct sun all year round to maintain the leaf hues. Plants bear dainty flowers on tall stems in spring or summer and they bloom for several weeks.

TEMPERATURE 5–27°C (41–80°F). Keep cool in winter.

LIGHT Position in bright light out of direct sun.

WATERING During the spring and summer, water when the top 2cm (¾in) of compost is dry. In autumn and winter, keep the compost almost dry, watering just enough to prevent the leaves shrivelling.

FEEDING Apply a half-strength liquid fertilizer once in spring.

COMPOST Plant in cactus compost, or a 50:50 mix of loam-based (John Innes No. 2) compost and 4mm grit.

FLOWERING This plant requires low temperatures of 5–15°C (41–59°F) in winter for flowers to form.

PROPAGATION Sow seed, or take offsets or leaf cuttings.

COMMON PROBLEMS These plants will rot in wet compost. Pests to look out for include mealybugs.

GRAPTOPETALUM BELLUM AGM

syn. *Tacitus bellus*
Chihuahua flower

The small, leafy rosettes of the Chihuahua flower look like grey-green water lily blooms. Its common name is derived from the clusters of pink and red flowers, each bloom of which resembles the pointed face of a chihuahua. The clusters appear on tall stems that grow out of the middle of the rosettes.

HEIGHT AND SPREAD Up to 8 x 10cm (3½ x 4in).

CARE NOTES: See above.

HAWORTHIA

A large and varied group of diminutive succulents, *Haworthia* have small, patterned foliage, which may be decorated with speckles, spots, stripes, or streaks. Some have smooth, chubby leaves; others are spiky with spiny tips. The flowers appear on long stems in summer, but are often green in colour and not very showy. They only appear on a few species grown as house plants.

TEMPERATURE 5–27°C (30–80°F)

LIGHT Position in full sun; place in light shade in summer.

WATERING During the spring and summer, water when the top 2cm (¾in) of compost is dry. In autumn and winter, keep the compost almost dry, watering just enough to prevent the leaves shrivelling.

FEEDING Apply a half-strength liquid fertilizer once in spring.

COMPOST Plant in cactus compost, or a 50:50 mix of loam-based (John Innes No. 2) compost and 4mm grit.

FLOWERING Flowers rarely appear on house plants.

PROPAGATION Take offsets or leaf cuttings.

COMMON PROBLEMS These plants will rot in wet compost. Look out for mealybugs.

HAWORTHIA ATTENUATA
f. CAESPITOSA AGM

syn. *Aloe attenuata*
Zebra plant; Fairy washboard

With its spiky dark green leaf rosettes covered with white tubercles (raised bumps) arranged in distinctive horizontal stripes, the zebra plant lives up to its name. The plant soon forms small clusters of rosettes and it flowers reliably each summer, the tiny green blooms held on long stems forming an elegant display.

HEIGHT AND SPREAD Up to 13 x 25cm (5 x 10in).

CARE NOTES See left.

CAUTION Wear cactus gloves when handling this plant.

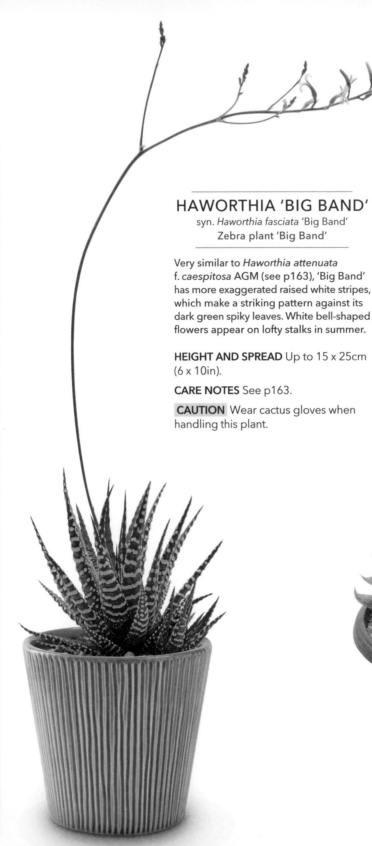

HAWORTHIA 'BIG BAND'

syn. *Haworthia fasciata* 'Big Band'
Zebra plant 'Big Band'

Very similar to *Haworthia attenuata* f. *caespitosa* AGM (see p163), 'Big Band' has more exaggerated raised white stripes, which make a striking pattern against its dark green spiky leaves. White bell-shaped flowers appear on lofty stalks in summer.

HEIGHT AND SPREAD Up to 15 x 25cm (6 x 10in).

CARE NOTES See p163.

CAUTION Wear cactus gloves when handling this plant.

HAWORTHIA CYMBIFORMIS 'GREY GHOST'

syn. *Haworthia fasciata* 'Grey Ghost';
Haworthia retusa 'Grey Ghost'
Window boats 'Grey Ghost'

You may find this elegant *Haworthia* listed under a range of synonyms, but the distinctive foliage of window boats 'Grey Ghost' makes it worth the search. The short thick triangular leaves, which are pale green with delicate white-grey markings, looks like they have been painted with a fine brush. Small white and green tubular flowers appear on long stems in summer.

HEIGHT AND SPREAD Up to 15 x 25cm (6 x 10in).

CARE NOTES See p163.

CAUTION Wear cactus gloves when handling this plant.

HOYA

These Asian climbers comprise a large and varied group originating in tropical forests, and include a range of plants that have the distinctive fleshy foliage associated with succulents. Many species are epiphytes, which means that they grow on trees, and the most popular house plant varieties are those with sweetly scented flowers. Most *Hoya* bear unusual heads of waxy star-shaped flowers which, in many species, emit a sweet fragrance. Place perfumed varieties in a large space, such as a hallway, where the heady scent can be enjoyed in passing; they may be a little overpowering in a smaller room.

TEMPERATURE 10-27°C (50-80°F)

LIGHT Position in good light out of direct sunlight, or place in light shade.

WATERING Water regularly from spring to autumn, allowing the surface of the compost to dry out between waterings. From late autumn to late winter reduce watering so that the compost almost dries out. *Hoya* prefer moderate humidity; stand the plant on a tray filled with pebbles and water to increase the moisture in the surrounding atmosphere.

FEEDING Apply a half-strength liquid fertilizer once a month from spring to late summer.

COMPOST Plant in cactus compost with extra perlite.

FLOWERING Flowers should develop when plants are given a little fertilizer. Do not move plants in bud, as the buds may drop off.

PROPAGATION Take leaf or stem cuttings.

COMMON PROBLEMS These plants are prone to rot if grown in wet compost. Look out for mealybugs.

HAWORTHIA TRUNCATA AGM
Truncate haworthia

The truncate haworthia may not be the prettiest plant in this group, but it is certainly one of the most unusual. It forms two rows of fleshy dark green leaves, the tops of which look like they have been cut off to form blunt tips. The small tubular flowers are greenish-white.

HEIGHT AND SPREAD Up to 10 x 20cm (4 x 8in).

CARE NOTES See p163.

HOYA CARNOSA 'TRICOLOR'
Wax plant

The flexible stems of this decorative climber can be trained on to a wire support or trellis for year-round interest. Grown for its colourful variegated leaves, which are green with cream and pink splashes, this hoya also features heads of small star-shaped waxy-looking white flowers with red centres. The blooms emit a rich sweet scent when they appear in summer, and each flower also produces a drop of nectar.

HEIGHT AND SPREAD Up to 1.8 x 0.6m (6 x 2ft).

CARE NOTES See left.

KALANCHOE

Natives of Madagascar and tropical Africa, some *Kalanchoe* species are large shrubs, but those grown as house plants are generally small- to medium-sized evergreen perennials. Popular for their bright, colourful flowers, plants generally bloom in late winter or spring, or at other times when grown indoors. The flowers are set off by the glossy green leaves or soft hairy foliage, depending on the species. You may also find plants with patterned or variegated leaves.

TEMPERATURE 10–27°C (50–80°F).

LIGHT Position in bright light but out of direct sun.

WATERING In spring and autumn, allow the top 2cm (¾in) of compost to dry out between waterings. In summer, allow just the surface of the compost to dry out before watering well. In winter, keep the compost just moist enough to prevent the leaves shrivelling.

FEEDING Feed with a half-strength liquid fertilizer once a month from late spring to early autumn.

COMPOST Plant in cactus compost, or a 50:50 mix of loam-based (John Innes No. 2) compost and 4mm grit.

FLOWERING *Kalanchoe* need a clear dormancy period in order to reflower. Prune back faded stems after they have flowered, reduce watering, and ensure plants spend 14 hours a day in darkness. This may occur naturally in winter, but if the blooms fade at other times, place a box over the plant. After 6 weeks, to stimulate flowering, bring the plant back into good light and resume normal watering.

PROPAGATION Sow stem cuttings.

COMMON PROBLEMS Prone to rot in wet compost. Check regularly for mealybugs and aphids.

KALANCHOE BLOSSFELDIANA AGM

syn. *Kalanchoe globulifera* var. *coccinea*
Flaming Katy

Dark green glossy leaves with scalloped edges provide the perfect foil for flaming Katy's bright starry flowers, which can last for many weeks or even months. They appear in late winter, spring, or summer and come in a range of colours, including red, orange, pink, white, or yellow. The double-flowered forms of this *Kalanchoe* resemble little rosebuds and are particularly attractive.

HEIGHT AND SPREAD Up to 30 x 30cm (12 x 12in).

CARE NOTES See left.

CAUTION All parts are poisonous if eaten.

KALANCHOE HUMILIS

syn. *Kalanchoe prasina*
Spotted kalanchoe; Pen wiper

Grown for its boldly patterned foliage, the spotted *Kalanchoe* produces grey–green wavy-edged oval leaves decorated with maroon spots and stripes. The older leaves on the lower part of the plant soon fall off to reveal the blue-green or purplish stem. Purple to green flowers appear in summer, but they are not very showy. Look out for the cultivar 'Desert Surprise', which has even brighter leaf markings.

HEIGHT AND SPREAD Up to 60 x 60cm (2 x 2ft).

CARE NOTES See left.

CAUTION All parts are poisonous if eaten.

KALANCHOE LACINIATA
Christmas tree plant;
Lace leaf kalanchoe

Tall and elegant, the Christmas tree plant forms a large shrub with slim, divided foliage that looks like the lacy leaves of a conifer. Clusters of bright yellow tubular flowers appear in early spring.

HEIGHT AND SPREAD 90 x 60cm (3 x 2ft).

CARE NOTES See opposite.

CAUTION All parts are poisonous if eaten.

KALANCHOE PUMILA AGM
syn. *Kalanchoe brevicaulis;*
Kalanchoe multiceps
Dwarf kalanchoe;
Flower dust plant

One of the smaller plants in this group, the dwarf kalanchoe produces graceful arching stems of silvery leaves that look like they have been dusted with white powder. In spring, clusters of tiny pink urn-shaped flowers appear on slim stems above the foliage.

HEIGHT AND SPREAD 20 x 20cm (8 x 8in).

CARE NOTES See opposite.

CAUTION All parts are poisonous if eaten.

KALANCHOE THYRSIFLORA

syn. *Kalanchoe tetraphylla*
Paddle kalanchoe; Flapjacks

Unlike its cousins, which produce tall leafy stems, the paddle kalanchoe forms a stemless rosette of paddle-shaped foliage. With its large, rounded leaves in shades of grey-green and dark red, the plant resembles a colourful cabbage when young. Once established, it produces towering stems studded with small scented tubular yellow flowers; these blooms last for many months, but then the plant dies.

HEIGHT AND SPREAD Up to 90 x 60cm (3 x 2ft).

CARE NOTES See p166.

CAUTION All parts are poisonous if eaten.

KALANCHOE SEXANGULARIS

syn. *Kalanchoe rogersii;
Kawhoe rubinea*
Six-angled kalanchoe

Unusual square or ridged stems hold the six-angled kalanchoe's oval, scallop-edged foliage. The pretty green leaves are often tinged red, particularly along the margins of the older foliage, and clusters of bright yellow flowers appear on tall stems in spring.

HEIGHT AND SPREAD Up to 90 x 60cm (3 x 2ft).

CARE NOTES See p166.

CAUTION All parts are poisonous if eaten.

KALANCHOE TOMENTOSA AGM

Panda plant

One of the most popular *Kalanchoe* species, the panda plant is prized for its velvety oval leaves. Grey-green and covered with silvery hair, the foliage also has brown spots on the leaf margins. It is grown more for its foliage than the small tubular yellow-green flowers, which rarely appear on house plants.

HEIGHT AND SPREAD Up to 90 x 60cm (3 x 2ft).

CARE NOTES See p166.

CAUTION All parts are poisonous if eaten.

KLEINIA

Some of these South African natives resemble cacti with spiny stems, while others are more shrub-like with bluish-green fleshy foliage, which may be deciduous or evergreen. A few species are popular for their showy red or white flowers, which usually appear in summer, but not many are grown as house plants. The most widely available is *Kleinia stapeliiformis* (see right), which has intricately patterned stems – you may find it under its old name, *Senecio*, with which it shares many similar characteristics.

TEMPERATURE 10–30°C (50–86°F).

LIGHT Position in full or filtered sun; provide some shade in summer.

WATERING From spring to early autumn, water when the surface of the compost is dry. Reduce watering in autumn and winter, keeping the compost just moist enough to prevent the stems shrivelling.

FEEDING Apply a half-strength cactus fertilizer once a month from spring to late summer.

COMPOST Plant in cactus compost, or a 50:50 mix of loam-based (John Innes No. 2) compost and 4mm grit.

FLOWERING Most plants will flower without any special treatment.

PROPAGATION Sow seed or take offsets.

COMMON PROBLEMS These plants are prone to rot if grown in wet compost. Check regularly for mealybugs.

KLEINIA STAPELIIFORMIS
syn. *Senecio stapeliiformis*
Pickle plant

The spiky ribbed pencil-like stems of the pickle plant, which are bluish-green with purple-green patterning, can be confused with those of a cactus. Slightly cascading when mature, they make a beautiful feature for a hanging basket, especially when the heads of thistle-like bright red to orange flowers heads appear in summer.

HEIGHT AND SPREAD Up to 25 x 20cm (10 x 8in).

CARE NOTES See left.

LITHOPS

Loved by children and very easy to grow, *Lithops* are commonly known as living stones due to their resemblance to little rocks or pebbles. There are many species to choose from, but all produce tiny fat pairs of stemless leaves that are fused down the centre to produce their characteristic stone-like appearance. The foliage is generally in shades of cream, grey, or brown and the different species are distinguished by their patterns or speckles. In winter, new leaves develop and then push out between the existing foliage pairs in spring, at which point the older leaves will wither. Daisy-like flowers, which may be scented, emerge in summer or autumn.

TEMPERATURE 5–30°C (41–86°F); will tolerate -5°C (23°F) for short periods if the soil is dry.

LIGHT Position in full sun; provide light shade in midsummer.

WATERING From spring to early autumn, after the old leaves have withered, water when the surface of the compost is dry. Stop watering after flowering and keep the compost dry from late autumn to late winter.

FEEDING Apply a half-strength cactus fertilizer once in spring.

COMPOST Plant in cactus compost, or a 50:50 mix of loam-based (John Innes No. 2) compost and 4mm grit.

FLOWERING Start watering when the old leaves die off and provide a little fertilizer to encourage flowering.

PROPAGATION Sow seed.

COMMON PROBLEMS These plants will rot if grown in wet compost; overwatering can also cause the leaves to split open. Check regularly for mealybugs and aphids.

LITHOPS KARASMONTANA AGM

Karas Mountains living stone

Originally from Namibia, the Karas Mountains living stone has pale beige or bluish-grey leaves, decorated with brown patterns that look like a cracked glaze. Satiny white flowers appear in late summer or early autumn.

HEIGHT AND SPREAD 4 x 8cm (1½ x 3in).

CARE NOTES See left.

LITHOPS MARMORATA

Living stone

The grey-white or pale grey-green leaves of this living stone, which sometimes have a purplish flush, are mottled with a white marbled effect. In late summer or autumn, yellow-centred white flowers appear, which look like little daisies emerging from between the stone-like leaves.

HEIGHT AND SPREAD 4 x 8cm (1½ x 3in).

CARE NOTES See left.

LITHOPS SALICOLA AGM
Salt-dwelling living stone

The salt-dwelling living stone has olive-green leaves decorated with an olive-brown lacy pattern on the upper surfaces. In some plants, this pattern is outlined in beige, so that the olive area looks like it is glowing. Daisy-like white flowers appear in late summer. Despite this plant's common name, it should be watered with fresh water, as you would do for the other members of the *Lithops* family.

HEIGHT AND SPREAD 4 x 8cm (1½ x 3in).

CARE NOTES See opposite.

LITHOPS PSEUDOTRUNCATELLA AGM
Truncate living stone

The truncate living stone has pale grey or buff-coloured leaves and an intricate spidery olive-brown pattern with matching spots on the upper surface. Sunny yellow blooms appear in summer or autumn.

HEIGHT AND SPREAD 4 x 8cm (1½ x 3in).

CARE NOTES See opposite.

ORBEA

Known for their unusual starfish-shaped flowers, *Orbea* have thick leafless stems that are often edged with spiny teeth or wide thorns. Another feature that will attract attention is the blooms' putrid scent. Designed to attract flies, they smell of dung or rotting flesh, and for this reason many people grow them outside during the flowering period in summer and autumn.

TEMPERATURE 5–30°C (41–86°F).

LIGHT Position in full sun but provide some shade in summer.

WATERING Water regularly from spring to autumn, allowing the surface of the compost to dry out between waterings. From late autumn to late winter, reduce watering so the compost is almost dry but the stems do not wrinkle. Provide good air circulation.

FEEDING Apply a half-strength cactus fertilizer once a month from spring to late summer.

COMPOST Plant in cactus compost, or a 50:50 mix of loam-based (John Innes No. 2) compost and 4mm grit.

FLOWERING Start watering in spring. Apply a little fertilizer to encourage flowering.

PROPAGATION Sow seed or take stem cuttings.

COMMON PROBLEMS These plants are prone to rot if grown in wet compost. Check regularly for mealybugs.

ORBEA VARIEGATA AGM

syn. *Caralluma variegata; Stapelia marmoratum*
Star flower

One of the most popular *Orbea* species, the star flower has long slim block-shaped stems with soft-tipped teeth along each of the edges. Relatively unassuming for most of the year, in summer it puts on a stellar performance when up to five large star-shaped purple-spotted white flowers appear. The blooms look amazing but smell horrible.

HEIGHT AND SPREAD Up to 25 x 25cm (10 x 10in).

CARE NOTES See above.

CAUTION This plant is toxic if eaten. Wear cactus gloves when handling this plant.

PACHYPHYTUM

Chubby-leaved and colourful, *Pachyphytum* are small slow-growing succulents, ideal for a mixed windowsill display. The leaves, which form little rosettes, may be tubular or round like pebbles, and come in a range of colours. Take care not to handle the plants, as the oil or pearlescent coating on the foliage is easily marked by fingerprints. The pretty leaves make up for the small bell-shaped flowers, which are quite plain in some species, and appear in spring and summer.

TEMPERATURE 5–30°C (41–86°F); will tolerate -5°C (23°F) for short periods if soil is dry.

LIGHT Position in full sun but provide some shade in summer.

WATERING Water regularly from springto autumn, allowing the surface of the compost to dry out between waterings. From late autumn to late winter, keep the compost almost dry, watering just occasionally to prevent the leaves shrivelling.

FEEDING Apply a half-strength cactus fertilizer once a year in spring.

COMPOST Plant in cactus compost, or a 50:50 mix of loam-based (John Innes No. 2) compost and 4mm grit.

FLOWERING Water in the growing season to encourage blooming.

PROPAGATION Sow seed or take offsets.

COMMON PROBLEMS These plants are prone to rot if grown in wet compost. Check regularly for mealybugs.

PACHYPHYTUM COMPACTUM

syn. *Pachyphytum compactum* var. *compactum*
Little jewel

The torpedo-shaped leaves of the little jewel are olive-green with burgundy tips, and decorated with a delicate white marble pattern. Tall stems of pinkish-orange flowers with yellow centres appear in summer.

HEIGHT AND SPREAD Up to 30 x 15cm (12 x 6in).

CARE NOTES See opposite.

PACHYPHYTUM BRACTEOSUM

syn. *Echeveria bracteosa;*
Echeveria pachyphytum
Moonstones

Loose rosettes of silvery, pebble-shaped foliage give rise to this little succulent's common name. The leaves' shimmering colour and powdery texture are produced by a delicate coating that covers the plant and marks easily when touched, so take care when handling it. In spring, elegant bright red flowers open from silver buds coated with the same powdery film as the leaves.

HEIGHT AND SPREAD Up to 12 x 10cm (5 x 4in).

CARE NOTES See opposite.

PACHYPHYTUM HOOKERI

syn. *Echeveria hookeri*
Hooker's fat plant

The olive to blue-green cylindrical leaves of the Hooker's fat plant are like little fingers, while a white powdery coating looks as though the foliage has been dipped into icing sugar. The lower leaves often drop off as they age to reveal the stem beneath, and pinkish-red flowers appear at the top of tall stems in spring or summer.

HEIGHT AND SPREAD Up to 30 x 15cm (12 x 6in).

CARE NOTES See p173.

PACHYPHYTUM OVIFERUM AGM

Moonstones

Among the most popular of the *Pachyphytum* species, these moonstones (a few species have the same common name) have pebble-shaped pale blue-grey leaves. Their chalky coating makes them appear soft to the touch, but resist the temptation if you wish to avoid marking the surface. Reddish-orange flowers develop at the top of tall stems in spring.

HEIGHT AND SPREAD 10 x 30cm (4 x 12in).

CARE NOTES See p173.

PORTULACARIA

In its native South Africa, *Portulacaria* is commonly called an elephant bush because pachyderms consider the plant a delicacy. *Portulacaria* comprises a small group of shrubby plants, but only *Portulacaria afra* is grown as a house plant in cooler climes. The leaves are small and round, and either green or variegated. The plants produce little flowers, usually pink, in summer. They make architectural focal plants when grown indoors and, unlike most succulents, prefer a little shade, allowing you to grow them farther away from the window.

TEMPERATURE 5–30°C (41–86°F).

LIGHT Position out of direct sun in light shade.

WATERING Water regularly from spring to autumn, allowing the surface of the compost to dry out between waterings. From late autumn to late winter, keep the compost almost dry, watering just occasionally to prevent the leaves shrivelling.

FEEDING Apply a half-strength cactus fertilizer once in spring.

COMPOST Plant in cactus compost, or a 50:50 mix of loam-based (John Innes No. 2) compost and 4mm grit.

FLOWERING Flowers appear without any special treatment.

PROPAGATION Take stem cuttings.

COMMON PROBLEMS These plants are prone to rot if grown in wet compost. Check regularly for scale insects and mealybugs.

PORTULACARIA AFRA 'VARIEGATA'

syn. *Portulacaria afra* f. *foliis-variegatis*;
Crassula portulacaria
Elephant bush 'Variegata'

Sometimes confused with
Crassula ovata (see p145)
the elephant bush's round
leaves are smaller than
those of its close cousin.
Plain green species are
available but the eye-
catching 'Variegata' has
additional appeal, sporting pale
silvery green foliage with wide
cream margins, which contrast
beautifully with the dark red
spreading stems. In summer,
clusters of small pale pink flowers
appear at the tips of the stems.

HEIGHT AND SPREAD
Up to 60 x 90cm (2ft x 3ft).

CARE NOTES See opposite.

SANSEVIERIA

A great choice for anyone starting a collection of house plants, few species are easier to grow than *Sansevieria*. Originally from Africa and Southern Asia, they are grown for their spear-shaped or cylindrical green foliage, which in most widely available cultivars features yellow and white stripes and patterns. Many *Sansevieria* are also good for the home environment as they absorb air pollutants. The greenish-white or cream-coloured flowers, which look like spidery lilies, are rarely produced on plants grown indoors.

TEMPERATURE 10–27°C (50–80°F)

LIGHT Position in a bright area out of direct sun, or in light shade.

WATERING Water regularly from spring to autumn, allowing the surface of the compost to dry out between waterings. From late autumn to late winter, keep the compost almost dry, watering just occasionally to prevent the leaves shrivelling.

FEEDING Apply a half-strength cactus fertilizer once a year in spring.

COMPOST Plant in cactus compost, or a 3:1 mix of loam-based (John Innes No. 2) compost and 4mm grit.

FLOWERING Flowers rarely appear on house plants.

PROPAGATION Take offsets.

COMMON PROBLEMS These plants are prone to rot if grown in wet compost. Check regularly for mealybugs.

SANSEVIERIA CYLINDRICA
African spear; Cylindrical snake plant

Less well-known than its cousin (see right), the African spear produces long poker-like tubular leaves, which are dark green with paler green horizontal bands.

HEIGHT AND SPREAD 75 x 30cm (30 x 12in).

CARE NOTES See left.

CAUTION This plant is toxic if eaten.

SANSEVIERIA TRIFASCIATA
Snake plant; Mother-in-law's tongue

The tall sword-shaped leaves of the snake plant are dark green and form a tight rosette. Look out for variegated cultivars such as 'Laurentii', which has yellow-edged dark green leaves and silvery white horizontal bands. Greenish-white flowers may appear in spring or summer.

HEIGHT AND SPREAD 75 x 30cm (30 x 12in).

CARE NOTES See left.

CAUTION This plant is toxic if eaten.

SEDUM

Known collectively as stonecrops, *Sedum* comprise a huge range of species, including many hardy garden plants and some tender African and South American natives that are best grown indoors in cooler climes. All species feature fleshy succulent leaves, which come in a variety of shapes and colours. The house plants include decorative trailing types and small upright species ideal for a windowsill collection. While the leaves are the main attraction, *Sedum* also produce clusters of tiny starry flowers in summer or early autumn.

TEMPERATURE 5–30°C (41–86°F)

LIGHT Position in full sun but provide some shade in summer.

WATERING Water regularly from spring to early autumn, allowing the top 1cm (½in) of the compost to dry out between waterings. From autumn to late winter, keep the compost almost dry, watering just occasionally to prevent the leaves shrivelling.

FEEDING Apply a half-strength cactus fertilizer once every 6 weeks in spring and summer.

COMPOST Plant in cactus compost, or a 50:50 mix of loam-based (John Innes No. 2) compost and 4mm grit.

FLOWERING Plants will flower without any special treatment.

PROPAGATION Take offsets or stem or leaf cuttings.

COMMON PROBLEMS These plants are prone to rot if grown in wet compost. Check regularly for mealybugs.

SEDUM BURRITO
Burro's tail; Donkey's tail

A popular trailing house plant, the burro's tail will add texture and interest to a hanging basket display. Its flexible stems are covered with small spherical grey-green leaves that overlap like the hairs on a donkey's tail. The foliage may turn purplish pink when the plant is grown in strong sun. Little pink flowers appear at the tips of the stems in summer, adding hints of colour to the overall textured effect. Take care when moving this plant, as the leaves are prone to fall off, although this does little harm to the plant, and the foliage can then be used for cuttings.

HEIGHT AND SPREAD 10 x 30cm (4 x 12in).

CARE NOTES See left.

SEDUM MORGANIANUM AGM
Donkey's tail; Burro's tail

Almost indistinguishable from its close cousin, *Sedum burrito*, this species has slightly slimmer teardrop-shaped blue-green leaves. In summer it too produces small pink to red flowers at the tip of the stems.

HEIGHT AND SPREAD 10 x 30cm (4 x 12in).

CARE NOTES See left.

SEDUM PACHYPHYLLUM
Blue jelly bean; Many fingers

The blue jelly bean quickly fills a pot with its sprawling stems of silvery blue-green cylindrical leaves, which resemble chubby little fingers, hence its other common name. The foliage turns pink at the tips in winter and sometimes throughout the year, while large sprays of starry buttercup-yellow flowers appear in summer.

HEIGHT AND SPREAD Up to 30 x 30cm (12 x 12in).

CARE NOTES See p177.

SEDUM x RUBROTINCTUM AGM
Banana cactus; Jelly bean plant

Upright stems of little banana-shaped leaves give rise to this sedum's common name, although they are blue-green with reddish tips, rather than yellow. The stems eventually start to trail slightly as the plant matures. As with other *Sedum* plants, display it where the stems will not be disturbed, as the leaves fall off easily. Small star-shaped flowers appear in summer.

HEIGHT AND SPREAD Up to 10 x 20cm (4 x 8in).

CARE NOTES See p177.

SEMPERVIVUM

The intricate leaf rosettes of these alpine species look like little flower heads or cabbages, and the wide range of colours offers something for everyone. Some species are covered with a fine woolly webbing, others have smooth glossy foliage, while the leaves of a few types are protected by a powdery coating. In summer, a stout stem will push out from the centre of mature leaf rosettes. The starry flowers bloom at the top of this stem, after which that rosette dies, but there are usually a few offshoots growing around it to take its place.

TEMPERATURE -15–30°C (5–86°F).

WATERING Water regularly from spring to early autumn, allowing the top 1cm (½in) of the compost to dry out between waterings. From autumn to late winter, keep the compost almost dry, watering just occasionally to prevent the leaves shrivelling.

FEEDING Apply a half-strength cactus fertilizer once a month in spring and summer.

COMPOST Plant in cactus compost, or a 50:50 mix of loam-based (John Innes No. 2) compost and 4mm grit.

FLOWERING Plants will flower without any special treatment.

PROPAGATION Take offsets.

COMMON PROBLEMS These plants will rot if grown in wet compost. Check regularly for mealybugs and vine weevils.

SEMPERVIVUM ARACHNOIDEUM AGM
Cobweb houseleek

Highly prized for its woolly coating, the cobweb houseleek is a favourite among collectors, and just as easy to grow as the rest of the *Sempervivum* species. The leaves are green or reddish-green and it produces starry pink flowers.

HEIGHT AND SPREAD Up to 10 x 10cm (4 x 4in).

CARE NOTES See left. Take care when planting not to get compost caught on the webbing. It will be difficult to remove.

SEMPERVIVUM CALCAREUM 'GUILLAUMES' AGM
Houseleek 'Guillaumes'

Originally from the Alps of France and Italy, the leaves of this decorative little succulent are an eye-catching combination of apple green with dark burgundy red tips. The pretty leaf rosettes make up for the pale green flowers, which are not as showy as those produced by some other *Sempervivum* species.

HEIGHT AND SPREAD Up to 10 x 10cm (4 x 4in).

CARE NOTES See left.

SEMPERVIVUM 'OTHELLO' AGM
Houseleek 'Othello'

This sought-after cultivar adds a moody note with its dark red leaf rosettes. In summer, the pink flowers on tall stems provide an exciting colour contrast.

HEIGHT AND SPREAD Up to 10 x 10cm (4 x 4in).

CARE NOTES See p179.

SEMPERVIVUM TECTORUM AGM
syn. *Sempervivum arvernense*;
Sempervivum densum
Houseleek; St Patrick's cabbage

This vigorous species will soon form a large clump of blue-green rosettes, suffused with reddish-purple tints around the edges. Starry purple-pink flowers appear on tall stems in summer.

HEIGHT AND SPREAD Up to 10 x 20cm (4 x 8in).

CARE NOTES See p179.

SENECIO

There are a number of tender senecio species in this large group of plants that are ideal for growing indoors in cool countries. They hail from areas of the world with a Mediterranean climate, and many have silvery leaves, while the foliage of some is covered with fine hairs that protect the plants from strong sun and drought. Daisy-like or fluffy looking flowers appear in summer and are usually yellow, or white in some of the trailing tender species. Many *Senecio* have now been reclassified under different species, but they may still appear for sale under their old name.

TEMPERATURE 5–30°C (41–86°F); will tolerate -5°C (23°F) for short periods if soil is dry.

LIGHT Position in full sun but provide some shade in summer.

WATERING Water regularly from spring to early autumn, allowing the top 1cm (½in) of the compost to dry out between waterings. From autumn to late winter, keep the compost almost dry, watering just enough to prevent the leaves shrivelling.

FEEDING Apply a half-strength cactus fertilizer once every 6 weeks in spring and summer.

COMPOST Plant in cactus compost, or a 50:50 mix of loam-based (John Innes No. 2) compost and 4mm grit.

FLOWERING Plants will flower without any special treatment.

PROPAGATION Take stem or leaf cuttings.

COMMON PROBLEMS These plants are prone to rot if grown in wet compost. Check regularly for mealybugs and aphids.

SENECIO HERRIANUS
String of beads

This *Senecio* is confused with its near relation, *Curio rowleyanus* (see p149), which also shares the same common name. You can tell them apart because this string of beads produces wiry trailing stems covered with teardrop-shaped leaves, while the curio has round bead-like foliage. Display it in a hanging basket where you can admire the delicate foliage and its small, white flowers, which look like tiny feather dusters, when they appear in summer.

HEIGHT AND SPREAD 5 x 60cm (2 x 24in).

CARE NOTES See opposite.

CAUTION This plant is toxic if eaten.

SENECIO RADICANS
syn. *Curio radicans*
Creeping berries; String of bananas

Another *Senecio* that may be found under *Curio* when searching, creeping berries produces long, trailing stems covered with banana-shaped foliage, hence its other common name. It grows quickly and will soon form stems up to 60cm (2ft) in length or more, so hang it up high in a basket where the sun will shine through the semi-transparent leaves. White cinnamon-scented flowers appear in summer.

HEIGHT AND SPREAD Up to 10 x 90cm (4 x 36in).

CARE NOTES See opposite.

CAUTION This plant is toxic if eaten.

CARE AND CULTIVATION

GENERAL CARE

Caring for cacti and succulents is relatively straightforward, provided that you understand how to cater for their basic needs. This section will show you how to choose healthy plants and keep them in top condition. Combined with the the specific guidance provided in the Plant Profiles chapter (see pp76–181), this advice will help ensure that your cacti and succulents not only survive, but thrive for years to come.

PLANT CARE
TOOLS

Caring for cacti and succulents is fun, but it will be even easier – and safer – if you have the right tools for the job to hand. The equipment shown below will help you look after your plants throughout the year.

Small trowels
Use for mixing compost and filling pots

Watering can with narrow spout
Ideal for watering plants from above; the narrow spout helps to target compost and keep foliage dry

Secateurs
For pruning woody- or thick-stemmed plants

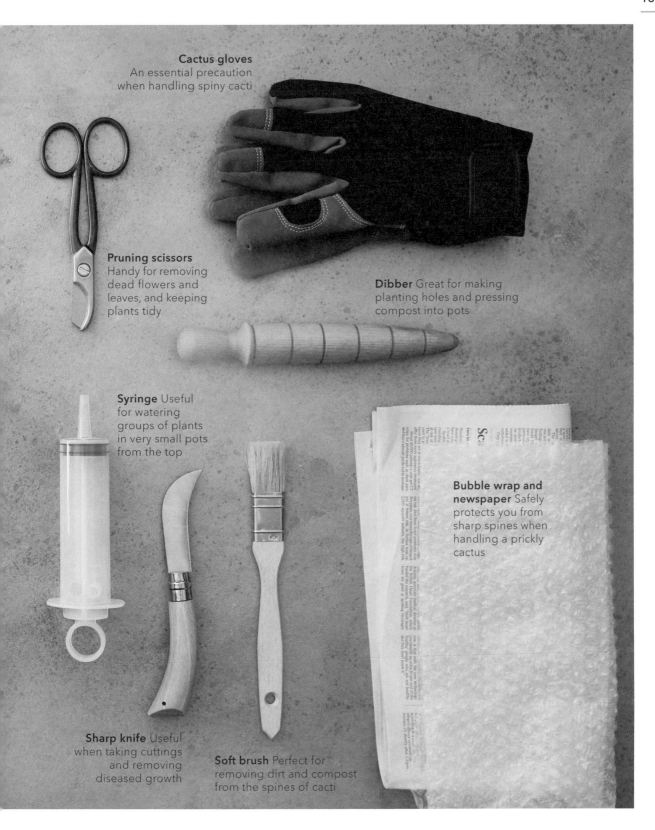

Cactus gloves
An essential precaution
when handling spiny cacti

Pruning scissors
Handy for removing
dead flowers and
leaves, and keeping
plants tidy

Dibber Great for making
planting holes and pressing
compost into pots

Syringe Useful
for watering
groups of plants
in very small pots
from the top

**Bubble wrap and
newspaper** Safely
protects you from
sharp spines when
handling a prickly
cactus

Sharp knife Useful
when taking cuttings
and removing
diseased growth

Soft brush Perfect for
removing dirt and compost
from the spines of cacti

BUYING AND HANDLING
NEW PLANTS

The array of cacti and succulents available from garden centres or nurseries can be very tempting, but before you buy anything, make sure your chosen plants are in good health and will thrive in the growing conditions your home provides. If buying prickly cacti or spiny succulents, take note of how to handle them (see right) to avoid injury or discomfort. Remember that some may have tiny hair-like spines that do not look vicious but break off and irritate the skin – check your choices in the Plant Profiles (pp76–181) to see if you need to take extra precautions.

GIVE YOUR PLANTS A HEALTHCHECK

Use this checklist when examining any plant you are considering buying, and put it back if it shows any signs of poor health (see pp210–17).

- Inspect stems and foliage for pests or pest damage.
- Look out for any yellowing or shrivelled growth, which could indicate a lack of water or nutrients.
- Beware of spindly or pale stems caused by poor light.
- Check for any brown marks or spots on stems or foliage; they could indicate disease or poor growing conditions (ask staff if unsure, as these marks may in some plants be a natural colouration.)
- Lift the plant out of its pot (if possible) to inspect the health of roots and look for pests.

IN THE SHOP

Think about where you would like to position new plants at home, and the growing conditions they will receive there. Researching a list of suitable plants before you go can be helpful (see Plant Profiles), or you can check plant labels and ask for advice from knowledgable nursery staff before buying to make sure that you can provide the plant with the environment it needs to flourish. If you are considering a really spiny cactus or succulent, think about the safety of small children, pets, and anyone moving around the house. When you've made your selection, check each plant over carefully for any signs of ill-health (see above right) and look at the base of the pot for the presence of drainage holes.

TAKING YOUR PLANTS HOME

Wrap your plants in bubble wrap, cellophane, or paper before transporting them. This will not only help to protect the plant from damage, but also insulate it from any drop in temperature, especially during the winter months, when brief exposure to freezing conditions could potentially damage or even kill it. Avoid leaving plants in a baking hot car in summer, too. Pack the plants up securely in a sturdy box to keep them from harm during the journey home. Wounds and marks on stems can leave permanent scars and may also allow diseases to enter the plant tissue.

AT HOME

Gently unwrap the plants and inspect them for any signs of damage, removing any broken foliage or stems as needed. If a plant does not have a pot with drainage holes, repot it (see pp194–95). If the plants are in the middle of their growing season (see pp188–89) and their compost is dry, place them on a tray or saucer and water from above or below, as needed (see pp190–91). Dormant plants should not be watered. Finally, check each plant's care needs (see Plant Profiles) and find somewhere with the right light and temperature for it to flourish.

HOW TO HANDLE CACTI

Covered in spines, cacti and some succulents should always be handled with care. Spines can cause painful injuries if you don't protect yourself, but there are several simple precautions you can take to keep safe when handling these plants.

Cactus gloves
Made from a thick material, these gloves protect your hands from the sharp spines. Some gloves are coated with nitrile, which forms a barrier that helps to prevent finer spines coming into contact with skin. Pruning gauntlets can also be used if cactus gloves are unavailable. Always handle cacti gently, even when wearing gloves or gauntlets, as the spines might still puncture the fabric.

Bubble wrap or newspaper
Place a folded strip of bubble wrap around a cactus stem and the air pockets will grip the spines while keeping your hands safely out of reach. A strip of folded newspaper works in the same way, providing a cheap method of handling cacti that can be composted after use.

GROWTH AND
DORMANCY

Most cacti and succulents have distinct seasons of growth, followed by a period of slower growth or dormancy, dictated by the fluctuating temperature and light levels they would receive in their natural habitat. When growing indoors, heat levels in particular can remain relatively stable through the year, so it pays to learn your plants' specific needs and, if necessary, take steps to provide them with cooler conditions that mimic winter.

GROWING SEASON

This is the period from spring to early autumn during which many plant varieties experience active growth. The longer days and more intense light levels, together with the additional warmth, provide the ideal conditions for plants to put on new growth and, in some cases, flower.

DAYTIME CONDITIONS

Plants require plenty of sun and warmth during the spring and summer months, so place them relatively near a bright window where their needs will be met. However, they may scorch if displayed too close to a window that receives full, strong sunlight, especially in midsummer, when the light is strongest (see p212). Ensure that plants don't overheat when temperatures exceed 30°C (86°F), as many cacti and succulents will start to suffer (see p213), and may become dormant.

NIGHT-TIME CONDITIONS

Cacti and succulents need some fluctuation between daytime and night-time temperatures during their growing season, just as they would experience outdoors. Desert-dwelling types, for instance, typically require lower temperatures of between 13–19°C (55–66°F).

One room, two seasons
The illustration below shows the same plant-filled room, with a window letting in natural light, at two times of the year. The left-hand side shows summer light levels, with full sun near the window fading to light shade at the opposite side. On the right, during winter, the area of light nearest to the window has weakened to indirect sun, while the area furthest from the window is in full shade.

KEY

Full sun

Filtered sun

Light shade

Full shade

SUMMER SUN

Sedum and **Echinocereus**
These desert-dwelling prefer full sun, so keep them on or near a windowsill, but move them further back if they are at risk of being scorched.

Sanseviera
This leafy succulent can live in filtered sun or light shade, so does not need to be moved between summer and winter (see opposite).

Schlumbergera
As a tropical cactus, this plant needs light shade all year round, so keep it away from the bright summer sun.

OTHER GROWTH AND DORMANCY PATTERNS

While most plants grow and become dormant during the seasons described below, some follow a different pattern. Many epiphytic cacti (those that grow on trees in tropical habitats), such as *Epiphyllum* (see p86), *Rhipsalis* (see pp117–119), and *Schlumbergera* (see p120), are in active growth during autumn and spring, and flower in winter and early spring, when kept at around 10-15°C (50-59°F). They then become dormant during the summer. Always check the Plant Profiles to make sure that you are meeting your plant's light and temperature needs from one season to the next.

WINTER SUN

Sedum and Echinocereus
Position these plants as close to the window as possible during winter to ensure they still get plenty of sunlight, making sure that they aren't in cold draughts or near a radiator.

Schlumbergera
Move this plant a little closer to the window during winter, so that it is not left in full shade.

DORMANT SEASON

From the middle of autumn to the end of winter, shorter days and low temperatures prompt most cacti and succulents to stop growing. This is an important evolutionary adaptation, helping them to survive in their natural habitats and conserve energy, ready for the following year's growing season. Try to emulate these conditions indoors to keep your plants happy.

DAYTIME CONDITIONS

Keep plants cooler during this period, and reduce or stop watering, as recommended for your particular species in Plant Profiles (see pp76–181). Cacti and succulents may still need bright light during this time, so move them closer to the window so that they can make the most of the short days. Make sure they are not in cold draughts or too near a radiator (see p213), both of which could adversely affect plants kept on windowsills.

NIGHT-TIME CONDITIONS

As for the growing season, plants expect a nightly temperature drop during dormancy; many prefer around 10°C (50°F), while some can even cope with light frost if their compost is kept dry. On especially cold nights, do not shut plants on windowsills behind curtains, as the temperature beside the window could drop below freezing.

HOW TO WATER YOUR PLANTS

Cacti and succulents evolved to store water in their leaves, stems, and roots in order to survive periods of drought, when they would naturally go dormant (see pp188–89). When caring for your plants at home, learn how to mimic the dry and rainy seasons in their native habitats to keep them thriving year after year.

THE GOLDEN RULES OF WATERING

1 Check there are adequate drainage holes in pots.

2 Water only when the top of the compost feels dry.

3 Avoid overwatering; cacti and succulents will not suffer if they dry out for a period, but they will soon rot in wet compost.

4 Tip out any water lying in saucers or trays to prevent waterlogging.

5 Reduce watering desert types in autumn and stop in winter. Follow a similar regime for succulents, but add a litte water in winter.

6 Avoid splashing water onto leaves and stems.

7 Lift the pot just after watering and as it dries out. You will quickly learn to recognise the weight of a wet pot and one in need of watering.

WHEN TO WATER

Succulents and cacti typically need to be watered regularly during their growing season, and less often (or not at all) when they move into a period of dormancy. Precisely how much water they need, and when they need it, varies from plant to plant (see Plant Profiles, pp76–181). However, there are two general patterns of watering: one for desert-dwelling types, and another for tropical plants.

Desert plants
During the growing season (see pp188–89), water plants regularly whenever the top 1–2cm (½–¾in) of compost is dry. Reduce watering gradually in early autumn and, once plants are dormant, keep them completely dry or water only occasionally over winter in the case of leafy succulents, such as this echeveria, to prevent the foliage from shrivelling.

Autumn and winter-flowering plants
Cacti and succulents that flower in autumn and winter need more water during these seasons than most. However, they also have a dormant period when watering is reduced, so check your plant's specific needs in the Plant Profiles.

Epiphytic plants
Epiphytic cacti that hail from the tropics, such as *Rhipsalis* (see left), prefer to be kept moist year-round, although watering can be reduced during winter. While they do need more water than other cacti and succulents, they still need plenty of drainage; if their roots become waterlogged, they will quickly succumb to rot.

HOW TO WATER

Depending on the type of plant and how it is potted up, there are three different watering methods you can use. Always use rainwater or distilled water, because the minerals in tap water can cause damage. If possible, ensure it is tepid too, as chilled water could shock the plants.

Watering from above
Use a small watering can with a narrow spout to pour water onto the surface of the compost. Try to water the compost rather than the stems or leaves. Water in the morning or evening, because splashes of water can mark foliage or even scorch plants in bright sunlight.

Watering from below
Place the pot in a tray of water about 2cm (¾in) deep. Leave it for around 20 minutes or until you see the top of the compost darkening, then tip any remaining water away. This method suits plants with furry or bloom-covered foliage which would be damaged by overhead watering or those with stems covering the soil.

Watering using a syringe
Position the fine nozzle of the syringe over the compost and squeeze to apply small amounts of water that will be absorbed by the compost without splashing the leaves. This method is ideal for cacti and succulents in small pots or in group arrangements, where a watering can spout may be too wide to insert between the plants.

HOW MUCH IS TOO MUCH?

No matter what type of plant you have, always allow it to dry out between waterings. Cacti and succulents are designed to cope with dry periods, so a little under-watering will do them no harm. Shrivelling leaves or stems are a sign that your plant needs a drink.

Overwatering, on the other hand, can quickly lead to root rot and other potentially fatal diseases (see p213). Make sure that pots have drainage holes in their bases and that any water lying in saucers or trays after watering is quickly tipped away; this will prevent the roots becoming waterlogged.

MULCH MATTERS

Adding a thin layer of gravel mulch on top of the soil surface prevents the compost below from drying out too quickly. In addition, it stops the plant's foliage coming into direct contact with moist compost, which may cause rot to develop. A gravel mulch is also decorative and sets off plants that contrast well with the pale-coloured stones.

COMPOST AND CONTAINERS

Selecting a suitable compost and pot for your cactus or succulent is very easy, because most of them need the same free-draining conditions at their roots. Bear in mind that containers must have plenty of drainage holes in their bases and always use fresh compost to avoid transmitting pests and diseases. You may also need a few other growing media when repotting, so check the ideal mix for your particular plant (see Plant Profiles, pp76–181). You can recycle old containers but wash them in hot, soapy water before planting.

COMPOST FOR EPIPHYTIC CACTI

Epiphytic cacti are native to humid rainforests and prefer more moisture at their roots, as well as good drainage, which means that they need a different type of compost to suit their needs. Plant them in a specialist orchid compost. This is composed largely of bark, together with other ingredients that make it both free-draining and water-retentive.

WHAT'S IN CACTUS COMPOST?

In their natural environments, most cacti and succulents grow in soil where water from intermittent rainfall quickly drains away from their roots. Specialist cactus compost, available from garden centres, nurseries, and DIY stores, typically contains a mix of loam-based compost and either grit or sand. This emulates these free-draining conditions, reducing the risk of the plants' roots becoming waterlogged.

COMPOST COMPONENTS

Instead of buying commercial cactus compost, you can also use a 50:50 mixture of loam-based compost and grit to make your own free-draining medium for your plants.

Loam-based compost
This compost contains sterilized soil, often in combination with natural materials, such as coir, bark, and composted wood fibre. It may also contain some fertilizers. Always use loam-based compost rather than soil taken from your garden, which could contain weed seeds, pests, and diseases.

Horticultural grit
Available in a range of sizes, 4mm grit is most commonly used in cactus and succulent compost mixes. It helps to open up air and water channels in the compost, creating the free-draining conditions these plants love. Look out for Cornish grit, too: this is even finer than 4mm grit, and is ideal for desert-dwelling species.

POTS AND CONTAINERS

An indoor plant will spend its life in a pot, so make sure it grows and flourishes year after year by choosing one that is suitable for your cactus or succulent.

- **Material** Most house plants, including cacti and succulents, are potted up in plastic containers. These are thin and lightweight, allowing them to be slipped easily into decorative outer pots, known as "sleeves". Classic terracotta pots are also a good choice for cacti and succulents, as they draw moisture from compost and help to keep roots dry. Set them on waterproof saucers to avoid staining furnishings. Avoid metal pots, which will heat up when set in a sunny position, raising the compost's temperature and harming or potentially killing your plants.

- **Size** If you need to repot your plant (see pp194–95), select a container slightly deeper than the existing one and around 2–3cm (¾–1in) wider at the rim. Your plant should grow to fill it within 2–3 years, at which point it will need repotting again. Young plants bought in small pots may need repotting annually into a container one size larger.

- **Drainage** Always pot up your plants in containers with drainage holes in the bases, as these allow excess water to filter away from around the roots. Without drainage holes, excess water has nowhere to escape, and the compost will quickly become waterlogged. Wet compost is the biggest killer of cacti and succulents, as it rots the roots and the stems (see pp213). Stand your pot on a waterproof saucer, or place a dull plastic one inside a decorative "sleeve"; these will catch any drips after watering, and prevent them staining your furnishings.

Choose a pot with plenty of drainage holes to ensure the plant's roots do not become waterlogged.

OTHER POTTING MATERIALS

Depending on your plant's unique needs, you may need to add additional growing materials to the cactus compost mix in order to provide the ideal conditions for it to thrive.

Horticultural sand can be added to cactus compost instead of, or as well as, grit to increase drainage. Always used washed, sharp, fine-grade horticultural sand; builders' sand can contain high levels of lime that will damage your cacti and succulents.

Leafmould is a crumbly dark brown material made from decomposed leaves, and contains a number of essential plant nutrients. It also holds water well, making it a good addition to the potting material of plants that prefer slightly more moisture around their roots.

Gravel is applied on top of the compost in a thin layer, known as a "mulch" or "top-dressing". This helps to drain water away quickly from the base of the stems and helps to prevent rotting. It is also decorative and available in muted or brighter colours to contrast with your plants.

Perlite is a pale, light mineral which has expanded during heating to give it spongy texture. A useful material for opening up and improving the drainage of compost, it also retains water and releases it gradually, which can be helpful when taking cuttings or sowing seeds.

REPOTTING
YOUR PLANTS

Repotting helps to make sure your plant's roots have the right conditions to grow and thrive. You may need to transfer a plant into a new pot to provide it with adequate drainage, or if it has outgrown its current container and requires more space for the roots to expand. Follow these steps to find out how to repot your plants simply and effectively.

WHEN TO REPOT

Plants should be given a new pot when they outgrow their old one, which for cacti and succulents is usually every 2–3 years. As the plant grows, its roots fill the container until they become "root-bound", which means they are so compressed that they are no longer able to absorb enough water and nutrients to grow well. If a plant is showing signs of being root-bound (see below), it is ready for repotting.

IS MY PLANT ROOT-BOUND?
The following signs can indicate your plant is ready for repotting:

- Roots are emerging through drainage holes in the bottom of the pot (see below)
- When removed from its pot, the plant's roots are coiled and densely packed
- Poor growth or yellowing foliage
- Very dry compost, as roots take in all available water

HOW TO REPOT

If your cactus or succulent needs repotting, follow these simple steps to transfer it to a larger container. Remember to protect yourself from spiny species.

WHAT YOU WILL NEED

PLANT
- Root-bound plant

OTHER MATERIALS
- Weed-suppressing membrane or gauze, to prevent compost falling through the pot's drainage holes (optional)
- New pot one size larger than the old one with drainage holes
- Cactus compost (or other suitable compost)
- Grit or gravel, for top-dressing

TOOLS
- Spoon or small trowel
- Bubble wrap or cactus gloves (for handling spiny species)
- Sharp scissors
- Soft-bristled brush

1 Water the plant 2 days before repotting it. Cut a piece of weed-suppressing membrane or gauze large enough to cover the new pot's drainage holes, then place it the bottom of the pot. Holding the pot on its side, scoop in a few spoonfuls of compost, then set the pot down on its side.

2 Using bubble wrap or cactus gloves if necessary, remove the plant from its old pot and carefully discard any top dressing. Gently tease apart any compressed or coiled roots, then brush away the old compost around the edges of the root ball with your fingers.

3 Check the roots for any signs of pests and diseases (see pp212–17). If you notice any dead or damaged roots, remove them with sharp, clean scissors, and remove pests from the stem or leaves if you spot them.

4 Holding the part-filled pot on its side, gently place the roots of the plant on the surface of the compost. With a spoon or small trowel, carefully add more compost around the plant's root ball, making sure the stem is at the same depth as it was in its original pot. Firm the compost gently.

5 Use a brush to remove any compost from the plant's surface. Top-dress the compost with a grit or gravel mulch (see p191), which will help to keep the stem dry when watering and retain moisture in the compost. Allow the plant to settle in its new pot for a week or two before watering.

KEEPING YOUR PLANTS IN SHAPE

Most cacti and succulents are easy to care for and require very little maintenance, but a few will benefit from a little pruning from time to time. For some, this simply means removing old growth and dead, dying, or diseased stems and leaves. Tall succulents and some branched cacti may need to be cut back every year or two to produce a more pleasing shape, or to encourage bushier growth. Follow this advice when pruning your plants to keep them looking good and growing well.

WHY PRUNE?

Cutting back a plant has many benefits, including helping to stimulate new growth, lowering the risk of disease, and improving the plant's appearance. Take these steps to keep yours in peak condition.

1 Reduce the height of the plant to keep its size in check, and to encourage the growth of new shoots further down the stems you have cut.

2 Cut away dead or damaged stems to reduce the risk of disease setting it.

3 Remove young side shoots that are growing into the centre of the plant where they will not receive adequate space or light to develop well.

4 Trim back leggy, over-long stems to keep the plant compact and encourage bushier growth.

5 Thin out overcrowded stems to prevent them from rubbing against each other and becoming damaged, which could increase the risk of disease.

BEFORE

1 *Reduce height*

2 *Cut away dead stems*

3 *Remove young side shoots*

4 *Trim back long stems*

5 *Thin out overcrowded foliage*

AFTER

HOW TO PRUNE

For cacti and succulents such as crassulas (below), opuntias, and kalanchoes, you need just a few simple tools to prune them into shape.

WHAT YOU WILL NEED

PLANT
- Succulent or cactus for pruning

TOOLS
- Cloth, for cleaning tools
- Surgical spirit (rubbing alcohol)
- Secateurs or sharp scissors

1 Use a cloth soaked in surgical spirit to sterilize the blades of your cutting tools before use. This will prevent infections entering the plant when you make your cuts.

2 Inspect the health and shape of your plant to identify the areas you want to prune. Make the first cut, pruning just above a bud (bump on stem) or growth line. Continue making cuts, checking regularly to assess the plant's shape, until you are happy with its appearance.

PLANT MAINTAINANCE

Keeping plants clean and tidy helps them to look their best and stay healthy by improving their ability to absorb sunlight - vital for growth - and catching any pests and diseases before they become major problems. Follow the advice below to enjoy your plants for many years to come.

Check plants
Inspect your cacti and succulents every week or two for signs of poor growth, and pests or diseases (see pp212-17). Don't forget to check the roots as well as the leaves and stems if the plant looks unhealthy.

Clean foliage
Wipe shiny succulent leaves (not those with a delicate coating) with a soft cloth and dust cacti with a small paintbrush once a week to remove dust and dirt. As well as dulling the plant's appearance, dirt can prevent foliage absorbing enough light for the plant to thrive.

Remove dead foliage
Shrivelled, dead, or damaged leaves, flowers, and fruits, not only look unattractive, but can also be a point of entry for pests and diseases if they are not removed. Also dispose of any that fall on to the compost before they rot.

ENCOURAGING PLANTS TO FLOWER

With the right year-round care, many cacti and succulents can be encouraged to bloom indoors. Although there is no secret solution that guarantees flowering, you can encourage many mature plants to bloom in your home year after year as long as you keep them in good health.

CAN MY PLANT BLOOM?

Before you start thinking about encouraging your cactus or succulent to flower, take a moment to check whether or not it is possible.

NON-FLOWERING PLANTS

Even with the best care, some cactus and succulent species will not bloom when kept as house plants, as their natural conditions cannot be fully replicated indoors. Check the advice in the Plant Profiles (pp76–181) to see if your plant is likely to flower.

IMMATURE PLANTS

Some cacti and succulents will not flower until they reach a certain level of maturity, which can take many years for slow-growing plants. Obvious as it may seem, the easiest way to ensure that a plant is mature enough to bloom is to buy one that is already in flower. Once those flowers fade, continue to care for the plant and it should reward you with more blooms the following year.

GOLDEN RULES FOR HEALTHY PLANTS

1 Check the individual care needs of your plants in the Plant Profiles chapter (see pp74–181).

2 Use containers with drainage holes and allow the top of the compost to dry out before watering. Never leave plants standing in water.

3 Provide plants with the right temperature, depending on whether they are in growth or dormant. Make sure they have good ventilation in summer and keep them away from heaters in winter.

4 Position plants in the right amount of light, providing shading in summer if necessary.

5 Feed plants carefully with a specially formulated fertilizer for cacti and succulents (see right).

6 Keep plants free of dust and remove dead leaves and flowers, which may harbour fungal disease as they decay.

7 Inspect plants weekly for pests and diseases, and deal with them as quickly as possible if found (see pp214–17).

Echinocereus rigidissimus subsp. *rubispinus*

Gymnocalycium baldanium

Mammillaria guelzowiana 'Robustior'

Notocactus ottonis

Astrophytum capricorne AGM

HOW TO ENCOURAGE BLOOMING

Flowering is a an energy-consuming process that starts long before the first buds begin to form. In order to bloom, you need to ensure that your cacti and succulents have enough energy to start the process.

DORMANCY

Many cacti and succulents need to experience an annual period of dormancy (see p190–91), during which time they conserve their energy for the following growth season, which will include their flowering period. By adjusting your plants' light, temperature, and watering needs as advised in the Plant Profiles, you can give them that all-important rest, before they start into growth again and begin to form flower buds.

NUTRITION

Despite their reputation for thriving on neglect, most cacti and succulents need feeding during their growth period, because nutrients are quickly washed through their free-draining soil when watering. Feeding is only necessary during the plant's growing season (for most, this is from spring to early autumn) when a diluted fertilizer (see right) should be applied once a month, or less frequently for some species. Reduce or refrain from feeding as the plant moves into a period of dormancy.

   Take care not to under- or overfeed plants, or to feed them during their dormant season, as this could lead to health issues, such as poor growth, yellowing leaves and stems, or excessive soft growth that will be prone to rotting (see p212–13).

WHAT IS FERTILIZER?

Fertilizer (also known as plant food) contains essential nutrients that plants need to survive. These include:

- **Nitrogen**, which encourages good growth, particularly of the stems. Cacti and succulents need a steady supply of this nutrient during spring and summer, because healthy leaf growth will increase the plant's ability to photosynthesize, thereby further strengthening the plant.
- **Phosphorous**, which promotes healthy root growth and is therefore a crucial aid for plants, helps them take in an adequate supply of water and nutrients from the soil. It also has a role in the production of flowers.
- **Potassium**, often known as "potash", also encourages strong, sturdy growth, as well as increasing resistance to disease. It plays an important role in the production of flowers and fruits, too.
- **Trace elements** comprise of a range of other nutrients that are needed in smaller quanties to keep plants healthy.

These nutrients are combined in varying proportions in different types of fertilizer, depending on the plant each has been designed to feed. Always opt for a specialist cactus and succulent fertilizer, which is specially formulated with the right balance of nutrients to feed your collection. Fertilizers are sold in liquid or powder form, which you normally dilute in water before applying, or as granules that are incorporated into the soil or compost. In all cases, follow the manufacturer's instructions, as well as those given in the Plant Profiles, before applying.

Mammilaria magallanii

Echinocereus viereckii subsp. *morricalii*

HOW TO
PROPAGATE AND GRAFT

Many cacti and succulents will grow new roots from leaves or stems taken from a healthy plant, which can then be potted on to produce new plants. Most of the propagation methods outlined on the next few pages are quick and easy, and ideal for beginners to try as they require no special tools or equipment. Grafting plants is a little more technical, but can be hugely rewarding.

WHICH PROPAGATION METHOD SHOULD I USE?

The leaf method is ideal for fleshy-leaved succulents, such as *Crassula*, *Echeveria*, *Kalanchoe*, and *Sedum* (see below).

The offset method suits a range of cacti and succulents including such as *Echinocactus*, *Gymnocalycium*, *Matucana*, *Mammillaria*, *Rebutia*, and *Aloe* (see p202)

The stem cutting method can be used for both woody-stemmed succulents, such as *Aeonium*, *Crassula*, *Sedum*, and *Kalanchoe* (see p203), and cacti with tall or trailing cacti like *Cleistocactus*, *Ferocactus*, *Opuntia*, and *Schlumbergera* (see pp204–05).

The seed method works for variety of cacti and some succulents (see pp206–07).

PROPAGATE FROM SUCCULENT LEAVES

One of the simplest propagation methods, this can produce rooted baby plants in as little as a few weeks. Always select plump, fully grown leaves that show no signs of disease or damage. The best time to take leaf cuttings is in spring when temperatures are on the rise, as cool conditions will slow down the process.

WHAT YOU WILL NEED

PLANT
- Succulent plant with fleshy leaves, such as an *Echeveria* (shown here), *Sedum*, *Crassula*, or *Kalanchoe*

OTHER MATERIALS
- Small plastic pots with drainage holes in the base
- Cactus compost, or a 50:50 mix of loam-based compost (John Innes No. 2) and 4mm grit

TOOLS
- Kitchen towel or plate
- Plastic container
- Cocktail sticks (optional)
- Watering can fitted with a rose attachment

1 Choose a plump, mature leaf from near the bottom of the plant's stem. Firmly tug the leaf to one side to detach it, ensuring the whole leaf comes away cleanly from the stem. Repeat until you have as many leaves as you would like to propagate.

2 Place the leaves on a tray or piece of kitchen towel and set them in a warm, dry area out of full sun for a few weeks to allow the base of each leaf to callus over. Do not water or mist them during this time. Roots and shoots may soon start to develop from the base of the leaves.

3 After a few weeks, pot up your leaves, even if they have not yet sprouted. Fill your pots with cactus compost. Carefully push the base of each leaf into the compost, gently burying any roots if they have sprouted. Prop up the leaves with cocktail sticks if necessary to stop them falling over.

4 Water often, keeping the compost moist but not wet. As the new plant develops, the original leaf will start to die off, at which point it can be removed. Once the new plant is established, repot it in a pot one size larger and follow its specific care advice (see Plant Profiles, pp76-181).

PROPAGATE FROM OFFSETS

Many mature cactus and succulent species develop offsets: little "babies" produced by a mature "mother" plant. Offsets can be removed and potted up easily to make new plants, offering a great way for beginners to increase a cactus or succulent collection without too much effort. Offsets should be taken in early spring for the best results.

1 Gently remove an offset from the mother plant. Small offsets can be pulled off easily with your hands (wearing gloves if necessary) or a pair of tweezers, while larger offsets may need to be cut away with a sharp knife.

2 Place the offsets in a warm, dry, shady area for about two weeks, or until the ends have callused over. Small roots may begin to appear but are not necessary at this stage for successful propagation.

WHAT YOU WILL NEED

PLANT
- Offset-producing cactus or succulent plant, such as *Mammillaria* (shown here), *Echinocactus*, *Gymnocalycium*, *Matucana*, *Rebutia*, and *Aloe*

OTHER MATERIALS
- Small plastic pots with drainage holes in the base
- Cactus compost, or a 50:50 mix of loam-based compost (John Innes No. 2) and 4mm grit

TOOLS
- Cactus gloves (optional)
- Tweezers or a sharp, clean knife (optional)
- Watering can fitted with a rose attachment

3 Fill the pots with cactus compost. Place one offset in each pot, so the base is in contact with the compost. Gently water them from above. Leave the offsets in a lightly shaded area to grow on, watering them only when the top 1cm (½in) of compost is dry. As the offsets mature, move them to a sunnier position and follow the relevant care instructions (see Plant Profiles, pp176–81).

PROPAGATE FROM **SUCCULENT STEMS**

Succulents with woody stems, such as aeoniums and some crassulas, are ideal for taking cuttings, while the fleshier stems of sedums and kalanchoes can also be propagated in this way. Stem cuttings are generally quick to root, producing new plants in no time. This propagation technique also helps to prune the "parent" plant, which will benefit from the process (see pp196-97) by developing more stems where those have been cut off and further down the stems. Take cuttings in spring.

WHAT YOU WILL NEED

PLANT
- Succulent with stems, such as *Aeonium* (shown here), *Crassula*, *Kalanchoe*, and *Sedum*

OTHER MATERIALS
- Plastic pots with drainage holes in the base
- Cactus compost, or a 50:50 mix of loam-based compost (John Innes No. 2) and 4mm grit

TOOLS
- Sharp, clean secateurs or scissors
- Watering can fitted with a rose attachment

1 Remove a leafy side stem at least 7-10cm (3-4in) from the "parent" plant. Strip away any lower leaves so that the bottom 2-3cm (1-1½in) of stem is clear. Repeat with several more cuttings.

2 Set the stems in a warm, dry area out of direct sunlight for a few weeks, until the ends callus over. Fill the pots with compost and gently insert one stem into each, so the leaves are just above the surface.

3 Place the cuttings in a plastic tray, water them, and allow to drain. Leave in a warm area out of direct sunlight, watering the cuttings when the top of the compost is just dry.

4 Once the plants take root and new growth develops above the surface, follow the relevant care instructions (see Plant Profiles, pp176-81).

PROPAGATE FROM **CACTUS STEMS**

This is a very simple method for propagating cacti, and can also help to save stems that have been damaged or are suffering from disease. The stem is removed and the healthy section repotted, allowing it to survive, while the damaged area is discarded. Of course, you can just take a healthy stem and use this for propagation too. Columnar cacti can be cut at any point along the stem, while segmented cacti stems, such as those of schlumbergeras and opuntias, should be cut where two segments meet. Take cuttings in early spring for the best chances of success.

WHAT YOU WILL NEED

PLANT
- Cactus with tall or trailing stems, such as *Cleistocactus* (shown here), *Ferocactus*, *Opuntia*, and *Schlumbergera*

OTHER MATERIALS
- Plastic pots with drainage holes in the base
- Cactus compost, or a 50:50 mix of loam-based compost (John Innes No. 2) and 4mm grit

TOOLS
- Bubble wrap or cactus gloves (optional)
- Clean, sharp secateurs
- Dibber
- Wooden sticks
- Watering can with a narrow spout

Damaged stem

1 Using bubble plastic or gloves if necessary, grip the chosen cactus stem and cut it from the plant with secateurs, ensuring the healthy cutting is at least 10cm (4in) long. If the stem is partially damaged or diseased, make the cut at least 4cm (2in) below the affected area.

2 Remove and dispose of the damaged area (if necessary). Place the cutting in a warm, dry, shady spot where the spines will not cause any damage. Leave it for around two weeks, or until until the cut end calluses over.

3 Once the cutting has fully callused over, fill a pot with cactus compost. Use a dibber to make a hole in the compost large enough to fit the base of the cutting.

5 If necessary, push a couple of wooden sticks into the soil to support the cutting and prevent it from toppling over. Water the compost then leave to drain. Place in a warm, dry, lightly shaded area indoors, watering only when the top 1cm (½in) of compost is dry. Once roots form and the cactus begins to grow, follow its specific care instructions (see Plant Profiles, pp76–181).

4 Insert the cutting into the hole in the compost so that 2½–5cm (1–2in) is beneath the surface, depending on the length of the cutting. Use the dibber to gently firm the compost around the cutting until it is secure.

PROPAGATE FROM
SEED

Cacti and some succulents are surprisingly easy to raise from seed, offering you a great way to increase your plant collection for very little outlay. Seeds can be sourced online or by visiting specialist nurseries. Depending on the variety, some seeds will germinate within a few weeks, while others can take up to a year, so patience may be required. Late winter or early spring is the best time to sow seed, if you have a heated propagator to keep them warm.

1 Fill the pots with cactus compost and firm gently. Sprinkle the seeds evenly over the surface; larger seeds may need covering with compost (check seed packs for sowing depths).

2 Place the pots in a large tray and part-fill the tray with water. Leave for 1 hour or until the surface of the compost darkens, showing it is damp, then remove the pots.

WHAT YOU WILL NEED

PLANT
- Cacti or succulent seeds

OTHER MATERIALS
- Small plastic pots with drainage holes in the base
- Cactus compost, or a 50:50 mix of loam-based compost (John Innes No. 2) and 4mm grit

TOOLS
- Tray, for watering
- Plant labels
- Watering can
- Propagator tray or clear plastic bag and rubber band
- Mister
- Spoon or small trowel

3 Label the pots with the name of the plant and the date the seed was sown. Transfer the seed pots to a propagator tray and cover with the clear plastic lid. If you do not have a propagator, cover the pots with a plastic bag secured with a rubber band. Place the pots or propagator in a shaded area indoors.

4 Leave the seeds to germinate. Remove the propagator lid or plastic bag daily for a brief period, wiping away any excess condensation. Mist the the surface of the compost if it becomes dry. As soon as seedlings appear, remove the lid or bag. Leave the seedlings to grow on, continuing to mist the surface every few days to keep the compost damp but not wet.

5 After a few months, the seedlings should be large enough to handle. Remove them from the pot and gently tease them apart, one seedling at a time, taking care not to tear the stem from the roots.

6 For each seedling, part-fill a clean pot with fresh cactus compost. Holding the pot on its side, lie the seedling down on the compost so that its roots reach into the pot. Carefully backfill with compost until the roots are covered and the seedling is secure but not buried.

7 Repeat steps 4–6 for the remaining pots of seedlings. Continue to mist them every few days, allowing the compost to dry out between waterings. Once the seedlings mature, follow the relevant care advice for your plant (see Plant Profiles, pp76–181).

HOW TO GRAFT CACTI

Not for the faint-hearted, grafting cacti is a little like plant surgery: the base ("rootstock") of one cactus is combined with a cutting ("scion") of another. The result is a unique living creation that, if successfully grafted, could thrive and even flower over many years. Grafting is a great way to accelerate the growth of a cactus that matures slowly by securing it onto one that grows quickly. Flat grafting (shown here) is the easiest method, and can be performed on columnar and round cacti with similar-diameter stems. For slim-stemmed cacti, try side grafting (see opposite). In all cases, for best results, choose two healthy cacti of roughly the same width

1 Make a horizontal cut through the rootstock at least 2.5cm (1in) below the growing point at the top.

2 Bevel the edges of the cut by slicing off 5mm (¼in) of skin at an angle around the stem's circumference. This prevents the inner flesh shrinking when it dries to a level below the hard skin, which will mean the rootstock will not fit snugly on the scion.

WHAT YOU WILL NEED

PLANTS

- Columnar cactus to be used as rootstock
- Round cactus to be used as scion

TOOLS

- Cactus gloves
- Sharp, clean knife
- Elastic bands
- Watering can with a narrow spout

3 Cut horizontally through the scion at the base. As with the rootstock, bevel off 5mm (¼in) of skin around the edge to help the plants fuse together well.

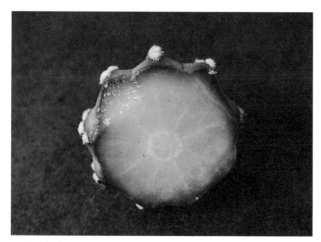

4 Both the scion and rootstock will have a ring
made up of tubes in the centre. These tubes
transport water and nutrients, and the rings of both
scion and rootstock must line up when they are
brought together. If the rings are not aligned, the
grafted plant will die.

SIDE GRAFTING

This variation of the basic technique is ideal for
grafting slim-stemmed cacti, which often have narrow
central rings. Cutting both plants at a shallow angle
exposes a larger area of the ring, making it easier to
line them up when uniting the rootstock and scion.

1 Using a clean knife cut the rootstock at an oblique
angle, about 2.5cm (1in) below the growing point, or
until the ring is clearly exposed. Cut away 5mm (¼in)
of skin all around the cut to bevel the edge (see Step 2,
opposite).

2 Cut through the scion near the base at a corresponding
angle and bevel the cut edge.

3 Press the cut surfaces together, aligning both rings and
removing air pockets. Secure in place with elastic bands
(see below), making sure you do not damage either
scion or rootstock in the process.

4 Support the grafted plants with a thin cane and twine if
necessary. Remove the bands when the scion has started
to show signs of active growth, usually after 4 weeks or so.

5 Align the cut surfaces and rotate the scion to
disperse air pockets. Secure in place with elastic
bands, making sure it is not too tight. Place in a warm,
humid area out of full sun – the humidity ensures the
flesh does not shrink back. Remove the bands at the
first sign of active growth (around 4 weeks).

PROBLEM SOLVING

If your plant isn't thriving the way it should, take a look through these pages to identify a cause and find a solution. More often than not, poor plant health is a result of insufficient or incorrect care. This can lead to a range of care-based problems, and can also increase the risk of attacks by pests and diseases.

TROUBLESHOOTING

Once you've identified the most likely cause of your plant's problem, turn to the following pages for the solution:

Care-based problems are the most common reason for ill-health in cacti and succulents (see pp212–13).

Pests are often hard to spot; check for signs of them regularly and remove any you find (see pp214–15).

Diseases can quickly take hold, so learn to identify their symptoms and how to treat them (see pp216–17).

WHAT'S WRONG WITH MY PLANT?

When one of your plants looks off-colour, refer to this simple chart to help you diagnose the problem. Be careful to check the whole plant for symptoms and, once you have identified the cause, take appropriate action. Issues with a plant's care are the most likely source of trouble (see pp212–13), so always attempt to remedy those first before moving on to more drastic measures.

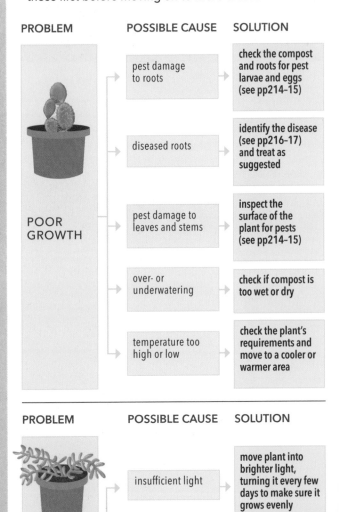

PROBLEM	POSSIBLE CAUSE	SOLUTION
POOR GROWTH	pest damage to roots	check the compost and roots for pest larvae and eggs (see pp214–15)
	diseased roots	identify the disease (see pp216–17) and treat as suggested
	pest damage to leaves and stems	inspect the surface of the plant for pests (see pp214–15)
	over- or underwatering	check if compost is too wet or dry
	temperature too high or low	check the plant's requirements and move to a cooler or warmer area

PROBLEM	POSSIBLE CAUSE	SOLUTION
DISTORTED GROWTH	insufficient light	move plant into brighter light, turning it every few days to make sure it grows evenly
	pest damage to new growth	inspect the whole plant for insect pests (see pp214–15)

PROBLEM	POSSIBLE CAUSE	SOLUTION
FLOWER BUDS FALL 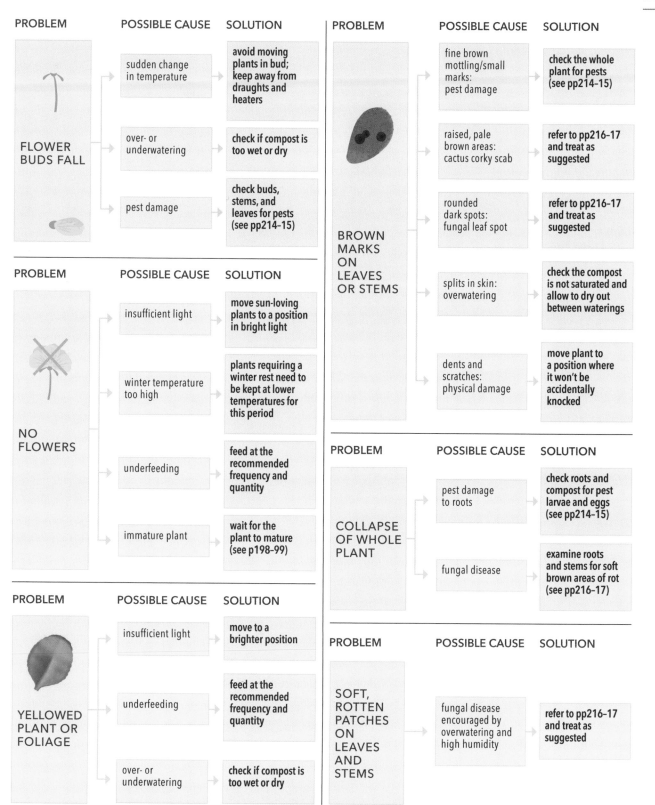	sudden change in temperature	avoid moving plants in bud; keep away from draughts and heaters
	over- or underwatering	check if compost is too wet or dry
	pest damage	check buds, stems, and leaves for pests (see pp214–15)

PROBLEM	POSSIBLE CAUSE	SOLUTION
NO FLOWERS	insufficient light	move sun-loving plants to a position in bright light
	winter temperature too high	plants requiring a winter rest need to be kept at lower temperatures for this period
	underfeeding	feed at the recommended frequency and quantity
	immature plant	wait for the plant to mature (see p198–99)

PROBLEM	POSSIBLE CAUSE	SOLUTION
YELLOWED PLANT OR FOLIAGE	insufficient light	move to a brighter position
	underfeeding	feed at the recommended frequency and quantity
	over- or underwatering	check if compost is too wet or dry

PROBLEM	POSSIBLE CAUSE	SOLUTION
BROWN MARKS ON LEAVES OR STEMS	fine brown mottling/small marks: pest damage	check the whole plant for pests (see pp214–15)
	raised, pale brown areas: cactus corky scab	refer to pp216–17 and treat as suggested
	rounded dark spots: fungal leaf spot	refer to pp216–17 and treat as suggested
	splits in skin: overwatering	check the compost is not saturated and allow to dry out between waterings
	dents and scratches: physical damage	move plant to a position where it won't be accidentally knocked

PROBLEM	POSSIBLE CAUSE	SOLUTION
COLLAPSE OF WHOLE PLANT	pest damage to roots	check roots and compost for pest larvae and eggs (see pp214–15)
	fungal disease	examine roots and stems for soft brown areas of rot (see pp216–17)

PROBLEM	POSSIBLE CAUSE	SOLUTION
SOFT, ROTTEN PATCHES ON LEAVES AND STEMS	fungal disease encouraged by overwatering and high humidity	refer to pp216–17 and treat as suggested

DEALING WITH
CARE-BASED PROBLEMS

The health of cacti and succulents is most likely to suffer as a result of the wrong care or growing conditions. Thankfully, these problems are often easily remedied if identified quickly. Use this guide to diagnose any issues you find and adjust your plant's care conditions accordingly. If there is no improvement after a few days, consult pp216–219 to see if a pest or disease may be responsible.

Scorched leaves are the result of too much strong sunlight

TOO WARM

THE PROBLEM Even in spring and summer, most cacti and succulents will stop growing at temperatures above 30°C (86°F) and all will be vulnerable to scorching (see opposite). High temperatures also cause compost to dry out faster, leading to underwatering (see right). Avoid heat from radiators below windows during the winter dormancy, when cooler conditions are needed.

THE SOLUTION Keep temperatures down by shading windows in summer with a net curtain or moving plants out of bright sun, and opening windows or doors to provide good ventilation. Move plants away from radiators and other direct heat sources.

TOO COLD

THE PROBLEM Low indoor temperatures will slow the growth of your plants, but fluctuations in temperature caused by cold draughts and shutting plants behind curtains at night can cause brown marks on the plant's body or foliage, flower buds to drop, or rotting if the compost is wet.

THE SOLUTION Protect plants from cold draughts and move them away from windowsills at night during winter. Check the minimum temperature limits for your plant (see Plant Profiles). Keep watering to a minimum or stop altogether in cool conditions, as recommended for your plant.

INSUFFICIENT LIGHT

THE PROBLEM Most cacti and succulents flourish in bright sunlight. Given too much shade, they will stretch towards the light and become "etiolated", with elongated, spindly growth that is washed-out or yellow in colour. Where light only comes from one direction, such as on a windowsill, plants can quickly become lopsided.

THE SOLUTION Ensure that your plant is given the correct light levels (see Plant Profiles). Move drawn-out, etiolated specimens to a brighter spot. Turn pots on windowsills every few days to avoid plants reaching towards the sunlight and becoming lopsided.

TOO MUCH LIGHT

THE PROBLEM Although most of these plants need full sun, even cacti and succulents can get sunburn. Their skin can be damaged, or "scorched", on hot, sunny late spring and summer days, causing affected areas to develop brown corky raised marks or white papery patches that turn pale brown. Epiphytic cacti require shadier conditions and will be especially damaged by bright sunlight.

THE SOLUTION Hang a net curtain over sunny windows during summer, but also on sunny days in late spring when new growth on plants is soft and prone to burning after their winter rest. Find epiphytic cacti a position with more diffuse light. Good air ventilation also helps to prevent scorching.

Too much shade will cause plants to become etiolated, while their foliage will look washed out

OVERFEEDING

THE PROBLEM Feed your plants too much and they will grow too fast. Although this doesn't sound like a bad thing, the soft, weak tissue produced by rapid growth is susceptible to rot and fungal diseases and may not flower well. Overfeeding can also cause "reverse osmosis", where nutrients are leached out of the plant into the surrounding compost, which could lead to signs of underfeeding (see below).

THE SOLUTION Feed plants according to their needs (see Plant Profiles). Make sure to use a specialist cactus and succulent fertilizer, which is weaker than standard plant food. Never feed your plant during its dormant period.

UNDERFEEDING

THE PROBLEM Pale or yellowing plants that put on little growth and don't flower are likely to be deficient in nutrients as a result of underfeeding.

THE SOLUTION Ensure your plants are adequately watered, because roots can't absorb nutrients from dry compost. Feed as recommended (see Plant Profiles), following the instructions carefully to avoid overfeeding (see below).

Underwatered cacti and succulents will eventually shrivel and stop growing

UNDERWATERING

THE PROBLEM Cacti and succulents are supremely adapted to arid environments, but eventually even they will suffer from a lack of water. Shrivelled, yellowing plants will eventually turn brown and die, but underwatering also results in poor or no growth, as well as bud drop in epiphytic cacti.

THE SOLUTION Check that your plant isn't root-bound (see p194) and repot if it is. Water plants sparingly from the bottom by setting pots in a shallow dish of water and removing it to drain when the top is glistening with water. This method will gradually remoisten very dry compost without waterlogging. Plants should plump up quickly, but lost buds will not be replaced until the following year.

OVERWATERING

THE PROBLEM Roots rot in constantly wet compost, which either causes the rest of the plant to turn yellow and die, or it can lead to the rot spreading and turning the plant's stem and foliage brown and soft. Too much water can also split the outer skins of cacti, leaving brown scars, or mark it with blisters or brown corky scab.

THE SOLUTION Check that the pot has drainage holes and is not standing in water. Remove your plant from its pot and leave it to dry on a tray or draining board. Once the roots are dry, cut away any that have rotted and repot the plant in fresh compost in a container with drainage holes; do not water again for a week after repotting. Always allow at least the surface of the compost to dry out between waterings and keep plants dry during winter dormancy.

Yellow stems and leaves can be a sign of underfeeding

Overwatered leaves will turn soft and yellow, and may start to rot

DEALING WITH PESTS

Given the opportunity, insect pests will happily make a home among the spines, furrowed stems, and tightly packed leaves of cacti and succulents. Left unchecked, they can quickly run amock, damaging or even killing off whole plants with ease. Pests can enter your home through open doors and windows, as well as via newly bought plants. Vigilance is key: familiarize yourself with the signs of pest infestation (right), thoroughly examine the stems, leaves, and roots of new plants before you allow them near the rest of your collection, and check all of your plants weekly so that if you do discover any unwanted visitors, they can be dealt with as soon as possible.

SCALE INSECTS

THE PROBLEM Small, brown, and limpet-like, scale insects grow to up to 1cm (½in) long, and hug tightly to stems and the undersides of leaves. Clusters of their white eggs may also be visible. They suck the plant's sap, causing poor, distorted growth, and can excrete sticky honeydew, which encourages sooty mould (see p216).

THE SOLUTION Inspect new plants carefully before buying and regularly check your own plants for scale, too. Where possible, remove scales by rubbing them off with your finger, or apply dilute solutions of soap-based products or methylated spirits with a cotton bud or brush (test on a small area first to ensure they will not damage the plant). Heavy infestations can be treated with a systemic pesticide.

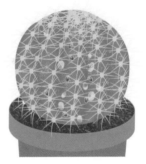

SPIDER MITES

THE PROBLEM These minute red, sap-sucking mites are barely visible, but can rapidly cause serious damage to plants or even kill them. They favour tender new growth, which quickly distorts and turns brown as they suck the sap, causing permanent scarring. Look out for tell-tale silky webs on plants.

THE SOLUTION Hot, dry conditions encourage spider mites: deter them by providing good ventilation and opening windows in warm weather. Remove and destroy infected parts of the plant or treat with a suitable pesticide. Infested plants are often best thrown away.

THRIPS

THE PROBLEM Almost invisible, these tiny insects, also known as thunder flies, are just 2mm (¹⁄₁₆in) long and suck the sap of plants. They are most easily spotted on flowers or flying around, but their wingless nymphs (juveniles) are even smaller. When feeding, they cause fine brown mottling on the plant surface, especially on young growth, and loss of colour or damage to flowers.

THE SOLUTION Use blue sticky traps around plants to trap the adult flying insects. Pesticides for use against thrips are also available.

> *"Open doors and windows are an easy way for pests to enter your home, but they can also arrive on newly bought plants."*

FUNGUS GNATS

THE PROBLEM Also known as sciarid flies, these small insects flit around the compost in pots and seed trays, feeding on rotting plant material and laying their eggs. Adult flies are merely a nuisance, but once their larvae hatch out, young gnats eat plant roots and can quickly kill seedlings and young plants. Damage to the roots of mature plants can also allow rots to set in.

THE SOLUTION Put up sticky yellow traps close to affected plants will catch adult flies.

MEALYBUGS

THE PROBLEM A waxy, white, cotton wool-like secretion conceals these pests, which look like tiny, light grey woodlice. They suck the sap of plants, affecting their growth and causing distortion. Their habit of lurking in the smallest gaps and crevices makes them difficult to remove. They also secrete sticky honeydew, which can collect on plant surfaces and lead to sooty mould (see p216).

THE SOLUTION Check plants carefully before purchase, because these insects multiply rapidly and spread easily to other plants. To treat mealybugs, contact insecticides that contain fatty acids or pyrethroids can be effective but they may need to be reapplied at suitable intervals (check the product label). Alternatively, prune out infected parts of the plant, or try pheromone lures to trap the adult males and disrupt breeding. Dispose of badly infested plants.

ROOT MEALYBUGS

THE PROBLEM If your plant stops growing and looks pale and sickly, knock it out of its pot and check carefully around the roots for woolly white clumps of small, woodlouse-like, sap-sucking insects similar to mealybugs.

THE SOLUTION Prevent root mealybugs becoming a problem by inspecting new plants before buying and checking the roots of plants regularly when you get them home. Remove the insects by washing as much soil as possible off the roots. Repot using fresh compost and a clean pot. Heavy infestations may be impossible to treat as no effective pesticides are available.

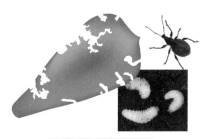

VINE WEEVILS

THE PROBLEM Resembling dull black beetles, adult vine weevils are about 1cm (½in) long and can be spotted crawling among foliage. They are largely harmless to cacti and succulents, but their cream, c-shaped, brown-headed grubs feed voraciously on fleshy roots and can quickly kill succulents such as echeveria.

THE SOLUTION Adult vine weevils move slowly, so catch and remove any that you see before they lay eggs in spring and summer. Check among roots for grubs when repotting or if plants look sickly and suddenly collapse. If grubs are found, use a hose to clean the roots and repot into fresh compost – do not water for a week after repotting. The nematode *Steinernema kraussei* is an effective biological control when applied in autumn.

DEALING WITH DISEASES

When it comes to plant diseases, prevention is always far better than cure. Poor care, such as lack of drainage or inadequate ventilation, can provide the ideal conditions for fungal spores to thrive, leading to many common diseases. Healthy plants are better equipped to fight off disease, though no plant can be made fully immune. If a cactus or succulent does shows signs of sickness, move it away from other plants immediately to prevent any infection spreading, repot it with fresh compost in a disinfected pot, and treat it as needed (see right). If spraying plants with fungicide, make sure to use a well-ventilated room, or go outside if it is not too cold.

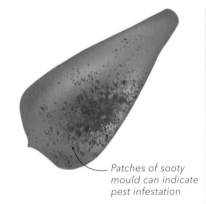

Patches of sooty mould can indicate pest infestation

SOOTY MOULD

THE PROBLEM A layer of black or dark brown fungal growth appears on the surface of leaves and stems. This occurs where sticky honeydew has been excreted onto the plant by sap-sucking insects, such as mealybugs (see p215), and it is a good indicator that a pest is also present.

THE SOLUTION Deal with the pest first, if possible, then wipe away sooty mould and honeydew using a soft cloth or cotton bud and warm water. There is no chemical control.

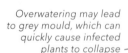

Overwatering may lead to grey mould, which can quickly cause infected plants to collapse

FUNGAL LEAF SPOT

THE PROBLEM Rounded brown or black spots appear on leaves or the plant's stem, spreading over its surface and causing scarring. They are the result of fungal infection, which occurs in humid conditions and where water has been splashed onto the plant.

THE SOLUTION Remove affected areas of the plant. To prevent reinfection, throw away any dead plant material in the pot, improve ventilation, and water from below (see p191) to avoid splashing the plant. Badly marked plants are best thrown away.

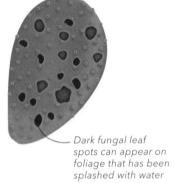

Dark fungal leaf spots can appear on foliage that has been splashed with water

GREY MOULD

THE PROBLEM Caused by the fungus *Botrytis cinerea*, this disease produces dark, water-soaked spots, particularly on fleshy succulents, which soon cover the whole plant, causing it to collapse. In moist conditions, infected areas become covered in dusty, grey mould. This fungal disease spreads in humid conditions and when water droplets splash onto plants.

THE SOLUTION Plants with some healthy growth may be saved by removing all diseased material and surrounding dead leaves and flowers that may harbour infection. Reduce humidity and water plants from below (see p191) to avoid spreading fungal spores. Badly affected plants should be thrown away. No chemical controls are available.

BASAL STEM ROT

THE PROBLEM Brown patches with a wet appearance and sometimes a bad smell develop at the base of the plant, close to the surface of the compost, and spread rapidly. The affected tissue becomes soft and the plant wilts, eventually collapsing completely. These rots can be caused by bacteria or fungi and occur when compost is wet, due to poor drainage or overwatering.

THE SOLUTION Due to the location of these rots at the base of the plant they are usually fatal, because the infected area can't be removed without destroying the plant. There are no chemical controls. Throw away infected plants and keep new plants in drier conditions.

ROOT ROT

THE PROBLEM Roots turn soft and brown or black, and once this fungal disease takes hold, the plant's stems and leaves receive no water from the roots and will shrivel and collapse. Poor drainage or prolonged overwatering will cause root rot to set in.

THE SOLUTION If caught early, try to save the plant by removing the dark, rotten roots and repotting the plant with fresh compost in a pot with drainage holes. Do not water for a week after repotting. If all roots are affected, the plant should be thrown away and care taken not to overwater any replacements.

Basal stem rot can rapidly cause plants to wilt and die

Root rot can cause a whole plant to collapse

DAMPING-OFF DISEASE

THE PROBLEM Seedlings (see pp209–10) rapidly develop brown rotten areas at their base, collapse, and die; this whole process may happen within a day or two. A white webbing of fungal growth then appears on the compost. This fungus often affects seedlings that have been sown too densely and where air circulation is poor.

THE SOLUTION This fungal infection is fatal, but can be prevented by sowing seed thinly in well-drained compost, and removing any lid or covering as soon as seedlings germinate, to maximize ventilation. There is no chemical control.

CORKY SCAB

THE PROBLEM Light brown patches appear on the surface of cacti, which gradually become raised to form scabs. While they will not damage the plant further, they are unsightly. Humidity, poor ventilation, over-watering, and possibly over-fertilizing contribute to the problem.

THE SOLUTION Increase air circulation around affected plants to reduce humidity, reduce watering and feeding, and grow in the recommended amount of light for your plant.

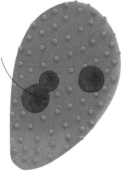

While not fatal, corky scab patches can look unsightly

INDEX

ACKNOWLEDGMENTS

Fran Bailey would like to thank all at DK, in particular Stephanie Farrow for giving her the opportunity to contribute to this book and Amy Slack for her unflagging support and word wizardry. Thank you also to Rob Streeter, Ruth Jenkinson, and Nigel Wright for their skill and expertise in bringing the book to life. Finally, thank you to the team at Forest and Fresh Flower for keeping the ship afloat in her absence.

Zia Allaway would like to thank the whole team at DK for their help in producing this stunning book, with particular thanks to editor Amy Slack for running the project so smoothly and checking the words, and to Christine Keilty and Sara Robin for their beautiful designs. Thanks also to photographer Rob Streeter and stylists Nigel Wright and Janice Browne of XAB Design for the beautiful images, and to Managing Editor Stephanie Farrow for commissioning her. Thanks to Daniel Jackson of Ottershaw Cacti for his help and advice, and for allowing the team to photograph his amazing plants, and to Christopher Young of the Royal Horticultural Society for his editorial help and for checking the facts. Zia would also like to thank her husband Brian North for his patience and support while she was writing this book.

DK would like to thank all the marvellous people who have helped make this book possible: Daniel Jackson of Ottershaw Cacti for welcoming us into his nursery and answering our many questions; Jan Browne of XAB design for her marvellous behind-the-scenes help with co-ordinating photoshoots and sourcing plants from across the country; the DK Delhi team for their tireless retouching work; Philippa Nash for her illustrations; Anne Fisher, Mandy Earey, and Jade Wheaton for design assistance; Poppy Blakiston Houston and Oreolu Grillo for editorial assistance; and Vanessa Bird for indexing.

ABOUT THE AUTHORS

Fran Bailey grew up on a cut flower nursery near York, where her Dutch father Jacob Verhoef encouraged her love of all things horticultural. After studying at the Welsh College Of Horticulture, she moved to London to work as a freelance florist. In 2006 she opened her first flower shop, The Fresh Flower Company, in South London. In 2013 she expanded into house plants with the opening of her award-winning shop Forest, which she runs with her daughters, and which is packed to the rafters with lush greenery. She co-authored her debut book, *RHS Practical House Plant Book*, with Zia Allaway in 2017.

Zia Allaway is an author, journalist, and qualified horticulturist who has written and edited a range of gardening books for the RHS and DK, including *RHS Practical House Plant Book* (with Fran Bailey), *RHS Encyclopedia of Plants and Flowers*, *RHS How to Grow Plants in Pots*, and *Indoor Edible Garden*. In addition, Zia writes a monthly column on garden design for *Homes and Gardens* magazine and is a regular contributor to the *Garden Design Journal*. She runs a consultancy service in Hertfordshire for people wishing to improve their gardens.

Christopher Young is the horticultural team leader of the Glasshouse at RHS Wisley, the Royal Horticultural Society's flagship garden in Surrey. He is a passionate plantsman with a particular interest in exotics and ferns, and is also a member of the RHS Tender Ornamental Plant Committee.

The Royal Horticultural Society is the UK's leading gardening charity dedicated to advancing horticulture and promoting good gardening. Its charitable work includes providing expert advice and information, training the next generation of gardeners, creating hands-on opportunities for children to grow plants and conducting research into plants, pests and environmental issues affecting gardeners.

For more information visit **www.rhs.org.uk** or call **020 3176 5800**.

Editor Amy Slack
Senior art editor Sara Robin
Designers Glenda Fisher and Harriet Yeomans
Senior jacket creative Nicola Powling
DTP designers Satish Chandra Gaur, Anurag Trivedi, Rajdeep Singh
Pre-production manager Sunil Sharma
Producer, pre-production David Almond
Senior producer Stephanie McConnell
Managing editor Stephanie Farrow
Managing art editor Christine Keilty
Art director Maxine Pedliham
Publisher Mary-Clare Jerram

Photographers Rob Streeter, Ruth Jenkinson
Photographic art director Nigel Wright

ROYAL HORTICULTURAL SOCIETY
Consultant Christopher Young
Editor Simon Maughan
Publisher Rae Spencer-Jones
Head of editorial Chris Young

First published in Great Britain in 2019 by
Dorling Kindersley Limited
80 Strand, London, WC2R 0RL

A CIP catalogue record for this book is available from the British Library.
ISBN: 978-0-2413-4114-8

Printed and bound in China

A WORLD OF IDEAS:
SEE ALL THERE IS TO KNOW

www.dk.com